CARING
FOR THE J CURVE

John Trotter

Credit Lines

Reprinted from *Black Elk Speaks*, John G. Neihardt, by permission of the University of Nebraska Press Copyright 2014 by the University of Nebraska Press.

From the book *Native American Wisdom*, copyright © 1991 by Kent Nerburn and Louise Mengelkoch. Reprinted with permission of New World Library, Novato, CA.

From the book *The Essential Rumi*, translations by Coleman Barks. Reprinted with permission of Coleman Barks.

William Stafford, *Ask Me* from *Ask Me: 100 Essential Poems*. Copyright © 1977, 2014 by William Stafford and the Estate of William Stafford. Used with the permission of The Permissions Company, Inc., on behalf of Graywolf Press.

Copyright © 1998 by Wendell Berry, from *A Timbered Choir: The Sabbath Poems 1979-1997*. Reprinted by permission of Counterpoint.

Copyright © 1990, 2010 by Wendell Berry, from *What Are People For?: Essays*. Reprinted by permission of Counterpoint.

Copyright © 1977 by Wendell Berry, from *The Unsettling of America*. Reprinted by permission of Counterpoint.

Reprinted from *World As Lover, World As Self* (2007) by Joanna Macy with permission of Parallax Press, Berkeley, California.

Alles wird wieder gross.../All will come again into its strength, Losch mir die Augen aus.../ Extinguish my eyes..., and *Was wirst du tun, Gott.../What will you do, God...* by Rainer Maria Rilke; from *RILKE'S BOOK OF HOURS* by Rainer Maria Rilke, translated by Anita Barrows and Joanna Macy, translation copyright © 1996 by Anita Barrows and Joanna Macy. Used by permission of Riverhead, an imprint of Penguin Publishing Group, a division of Penguin Random House LLC. All rights reserved.

ISBN: 978-1-54391-987-5 (print)
ISBN: 978-1-54391-988-2 (ebook)

TABLE OF CONTENTS

PREFACE

Introducing the Author and the Pieces

Disclaimer

I feel a bit like Rabbi Adin Steinsaltz must have felt when he spoke about his work on the Talmud. He said

> ... there was a feeling that there is something that has to be done. ... Now I know that I am not qualified, I am not the best person to do it, I am not the right person to do it, but I'm here. So in a way it is not hubris.[1]

Like Rabbi Steinsaltz, I have no sense that I'm the right person to write this. I have no qualification greater than my interest in the health and well-being of the Earth and care for great-grandchildren. I have only the deep sense that I'm here and this elephant needs to be outed.

My education is basically irrelevant and there's little particularly special about who I am or what I've done.[2] I'm a long-time supporter of Zero Population Growth (now Population Connection). I've read some books.[3] I tend to believe peer-reviewed science and agree with reasonable conclusions. But these Pieces carry weight only to the degree that they expand your understanding. After all, all this emerges through observation followed by reflection and so is subject to confirmation by your experience and reflection.

Intention

These five Pieces explore how I feel and care about the Earth, though I know the futility of that, for very little I read really changes my mind. In truth, I often dismiss other peoples' words or writing, or else I take them as confirmation of my own sense of things. Only rarely do they challenge me to rethink and reexamine my position, which I then may or may not do. So I present these Pieces as the sum of my experience, my curiosity, and my desire for a healthy Earth and I invite your similar consideration.

These Pieces present my sense that we live in intimate partnership with the Earth and all its creatures; that our best response to the Earth's fruitfulness is deep gratitude which leads to responsible service. I believe that being at the top of the intelligence chain means serving from a planet-wide point of view. And I want that planet-wide point of view to lead to a global dialog about quality of life for how many creatures and for what length of time.

Contents

This preface sets the context for the Five Pieces that follow:

- 1) Relations – our relationship with the Earth.
- 2) Implications – the implications of being human.
- 3) Issues – a survey of issues and discovery of a common factor.
- 4) Population – a discussion of the common factor.
- 5) POV Earth – plain talk from the Earth's point of view.

Approach

These Pieces are best read adagio—slowly, thoughtfully, critically. They present the opinion that the majority of our ecological and social issues have a common factor—so many people—and that any long-term solution includes fewer people. This is just an opinion, intended to open up discussion about population, the earth's carrying capacity, and our responsibility to the future. Such a discussion will be difficult, complex, and nuanced, best done with positions considered thoroughly but held flexibly so that everyone can be heard and respected. Listening is central to understanding.

Gabriel García Márquez once said transforming the incredible into the believable was a matter of telling it straight. As Marquez suggests, I have worked to keep these Pieces straight. I hope those places where I may have failed are both obvious and forgivable.

Endnote

Once I started to write, I was relieved to find as many others as concerned as there are and then dismayed to discover how ignorant I was. As soon as I started into research, my rant was shredded.

So I want to thank a *few* of those whose books and writings have supported my education: Wendell Berry, Dee Brown, Pat Buchanan, Carlo Cipolla, Joel Cohen, Meghan Daum, Ruth DeFries, Mei Fong, Martin Ford, Jonathan Haidt, Tim Jackson, Joanna Macy, Rainer Maria Rilke, Rumi, Nate Silver, Shel Silverstein, and Alan Weisman.

I have only been the organizer of these pieces, having in truth been supported by a vast cast of other authors, co-authors, co-writers, and co-contributors. Here is a partial list, in alphabetical order of last name (for my ease of mind):

Tom Burger, Heaven Edwards, Colleen Kelly, Julie-Ann and Tom Kosakowski, Lorraine Kumpf, Karen Maneely, Rosa Martinez, Roshi Wendy Nakao, Carol Schmitt, Judith Searle, Burt Wetanson, and members of the Zen Center of Los Angeles Brown-Green Circle.

I want this conversation about population care to be most tender, while being convincing of its necessity. My taking action is to offer these Pieces. Your taking action is yours.

FIRST PIECE

Our Relationship with the Earth

Infinite gratitude, infinite service, infinite responsibility[4]

INTENTION

This First Piece presents the opinion that we fit so naturally with the creatures and features of the Earth that life is a gift, as if of a higher power. It considers the relationship between Earth and human beings, suggesting that humans have stood in awe of the Earth as a source of life and nourishment, as an ineffable treasure. It suggests how to respond to this generosity, these blessings.

RELATIONSHIP

Whether you subscribe to evolution or to Creation, it's possible to agree that we live in intimate relationship with the Earth. All that we have, all that we are starts from the Earth; all that we use, all that we enjoy is harvest of the Earth; and all that we put down, all that we discard returns to the Earth. Indeed, as we venture into space this relationship expands to the stars. Whether you call it evidence of our grandeur or of our hubris, we have established a relationship throughout the universe, putting stuff onto the Moon, Mercury, Venus, Mars, Jupiter, and Saturn, onto a comet, and out of our solar system into the universe at large.

Evolutionists say that we co-evolved with the Earth over hundreds of thousands, if not millions, of years. Creationists say God brought us all into being in seven days. Either way, emergent or intricately, lovingly designed, we *fit and belong* here. We intermingle and interact naturally with all the other creatures and features of the planet. And though as individuals we are small compared to the Earth, the aggregate of what we do—whether through predestination or divine partnership or free will or random chance or unconscious indifference—matters.

THE EARTH–HUMAN RELATIONSHIP

Until recently the goodness of the Earth–human fit and the close balance between birth and death rates allowed us to view life in the biosphere as a virtually inexhaustible gift. (See Figure 2.1, "High Stationary", in the Second Piece). The air, water, soil, plants, and animals, and the Earth's ability to regenerate what we used and to absorb our wastes had stayed quite balanced. We lived this way for millennia, naming the planet Gaia, Mother Earth. If we thought of this at all, we thought of the Earth as a cornucopia.

Expressions of these blessings have emerged throughout the ages. The Bible, Native Americans, poets, religious leaders, and astronauts have all responded to these gifts, suggesting how we should consider them. Here are some of those expressions:

THE BIBLE

The Green Bible[5] has made a detailed study of the verses in the Bible that address the relationship between God and Creation. It begins with essays from respected theologians and conservationists and a collection called "Teachings on Creation through the Ages", such as:

- Irenaeus (120–202)

    The initial step for a soul to come to knowledge of God is contemplation of nature.

- Basil the Great (329–379), *Hexaemeron*, Homily V, "The Germination of the Earth".

    I want creation to penetrate you with so much admiration that wherever you go, the least plant may bring you the clear remembrance of the Creator.... One blade of grass or one speck of dust is enough to occupy your entire mind in beholding the art with which it has been made.

- Midrash Tanchuma, Kodashim 8 (fourth–fifth centuries)
    Even if you are old, you must plant. Just as you found trees planted by others, you must plant them for your children.
- Francis Schaeffer (1912–1984) *Pollution and the Death of Man*
    If I am going to be in the right relationship with God, I should treat the things he has made in the same way he treats them.
- Rick Warren (1954–) *The Purpose Driven Life*
    We cannot be all that God wants us to be without caring about the earth.

The Green Bible identifies over 1000 verses based on:

- how God and Jesus interact with, care for, and are intimately involved with all of creation,
- how all the elements of creation—land, water, air, plants, animals, human beings—are interdependent,
- how nature responds to God,
- how we are called to care for creation.

Besides these verses of environmental and ecological importance, *The Green Bible* includes a resource guide to ideas and organizations. This list includes:

- 27 denominational environmental programs,
- 3 denominational statements and activities, and
- 39 faith-based environmental organizations.

NATIVE AMERICANS

Native Americans have long been regarded as carrying a deep and abiding spiritual respect for the land and its plants and animals, taking only what is needed, using all that is taken, and expressing gratitude for it all.

- Chief Seattle, in his 1854 reply to President Pierce, said
    How can you buy or sell the sky, the warmth of the land? The idea is strange to us. If we do not own the freshness

of the air and the sparkle of the water, how can you buy them? Every part of this earth is sacred to my people. Every shining pine needle, every sandy shore, every mist in the dark woods, every clearing and humming insect is holy in the memory experience of my people.[6]

- Black Elk, an Oglala Sioux holy man, said this to John G. Neihardt in the book *Black Elk Speaks*:

    You have noticed that everything an Indian does is in a circle, and that is because The Power of the World always works in circles, and everything tries to be round. In the old days when we were a strong and happy people, all our power came to us from the sacred hoop of the nation, and so long as the hoop was unbroken, the people flourished. The flowering tree was the living center of the hoop, and the circle of the four quarters nourished it. The east gave peace and light, the south gave warmth, the west gave rain, and the north with its cold and mighty wind gave strength and endurance. This knowledge came to us from the outer world with our religion. Everything the Power of the World does is done in a circle. The sky is round, and I have heard that the earth is round like a ball, and so are all the stars. The wind, in its greatest power, whirls. Birds make their nests in circles, for theirs is the same religion as ours. The sun comes forth and goes down again in a circle. The moon does the same, and both are round. Even the seasons form a great circle in their changing, and always come back again to where they were. The life of a man is a circle from childhood to childhood, and so it is in everything where power moves.[7]

- From the Iroquois Constitution:

    The Onandaga [Iroquois] lords shall open each council by greeting their cousin lords, and expressing their gratitude to them. And they shall offer thanks to the earth where all people dwell—

To the streams of water, the pools, the springs, and the lakes; to the maize and the fruits—

To the medicinal herbs and the trees, to the forest trees for their usefulness, to the animals that serve as food and who offer their pelts as clothing—

To the great winds and the lesser winds; to the Thunderers; and the Sun, the mighty warrior; to the moon—

To the messengers of the Great Spirit who dwells in the skies above, who gives all things useful to men, who is the source and ruler of health and life. Then shall the Onandaga lords declare the council open.[8]

- From Chief Luther Standing Bear, Teton Sioux:

From Wakan Tanka, the Great Spirit, there came a great unifying life force that flowed in and through all things— the flowers of the plains, blowing winds, rocks, trees, birds, animals—and was the same force that had been breathed into the first man. Thus all things were kindred, and were brought together by the same Great Mystery.

Kinship with all creatures of the earth, sky, and water was a real and active principle. In the animal and bird world there existed a brotherly feeling that kept the Lakota safe among them. And so close did some of the Lakotas come to their feathered and furred friends that in true brotherhood they spoke a common tongue.

The animals had rights—the right of man's protection, the right to live, the right to multiply, the right to freedom, and the right to man's indebtedness—and in recognition of these rights the Lakota never enslaved an animal, and spared all life that was not needed for food and clothing. ...

The Lakota could despise no creature, for all were of one blood, made by the same hand, and filled with the essence of the Great Mystery. ...[9]

POETS

- Rumi writes poems from a God-saturated place, from a perspective of non-duality. In the poem *Father Reason* he expresses gratitude for this very moment:

  > The universe is a form of divine law,
  > your reasonable father.
  > When you feel ungrateful to him,
  > the shapes of the world seem mean and ugly.
  > Make peace with that father, the elegant patterning,
  > and every experience will fill with immediacy.
  > Because I love this, I am never bored.
  > Beauty constantly wells up, a noise of springwater
  > in my ear and in my inner being.
  > Tree limbs rise and fall like the ecstatic arms
  > of those who have submitted to the mystical life. ...
  > The conventional opinion of this poetry is,
  > it shows great optimism for the future.
  > But Father Reason says,
  > *No need to announce the future!*
  > This now is it. *This.* Your deepest need and desire
  > is satisfied by the *moment's* energy
  > here in your hand.[10]

- Similarly, Rilke, in II,7 of his *Book of Hours: Love Poems to God*, expresses his gratitude directly to God as loyal dedication:

  > Extinguish my eyes, I'll go on seeing you.
  > Seal my ears, I'll go on hearing you.
  > And without feet I can make my way to you,
  > without a mouth I can swear your name.
  > Break off my arms, I'll take hold of you
  > with my heart as with a hand.
  > Stop my heart, and my brain will start to beat.
  > And if you consume my brain with fire,
  > I'll feel you burn in every drop of my blood.[11]

- Walt Whitman writes in *Leaves of Grass*:

... The earth does not withhold, it is generous enough.

The truths of the earth continually wait, they are not so conceal'd either,

They are calm, subtle, untransmissible by print,

They are imbued through all things, conveying themselves willingly ...

The earth does not argue, is not pathetic, has no arrangements,

Does not scream, haste, persuade, threaten, promise,

Makes no discriminations, has no conceivable failures,

Closes nothing, refuses nothing, shuts none out.

Of all the powers, objects, states, it notifies, shuts none out.[12]

- Joanna Macy writes:

   Gratitude for the gift of life is the primary wellspring of all religions, the hallmark of the mystic, the source of all true art. Yet we so easily take this gift for granted. That is why so many spiritual traditions begin with thanksgiving, to remind us that for all our woes and worries, our existence itself is an unearned benefaction, which we could never of ourselves create.[13]

- William Stafford writes in his poem *Earth Dweller:*

   ... Now I know why people worship, carry around

   magic emblems, wake up talking dreams

   they teach to their children: the world speaks.

   The world speaks everything to us.

   It is our only friend.[14]

RELIGIOUS LEADERS

- *Ecclesiastes Rabbah* 7:13 (sixth–eighth centuries):

   See my works, how fine and excellent they are! All that I created, I created for you. Reflect on this, and do not corrupt or desolate my world; for if you do, there will be no one to repair it after you.[15]

- Martin Luther (1483–1546):

  God writes the gospel not in the Bible alone, but also on trees, and in the flowers and clouds and stars.[16]

- Billy Graham is quoted in the *Detroit Free Press*:

  To drive to extinction something He has created is wrong. He has a purpose for everything... We Christians have a responsibility to take the lead in caring for the earth.[17]

- Sallie McFague writes in *The Body of God*:

  We have defined our duties primarily in relationship to God (First Great Commandment) and secondarily in relationship to other human beings (Second Great Commandment)[18], but seldom in relationship to the earth, its creatures and its care. A first, sobering step, therefore, is to look at ourselves from the earth up rather than from the sky down. The postmodern scientific picture of reality will by no means tell us all we need to know about ourselves, but it will give us a base in reality (as understood in our time), so that whatever else we say about ourselves from the perspective of belonging to the body of God, a body overlain by the cosmic Christ, will be grounded, literally rooted, in the earth.[19]

- Wendell Berry, in Chapter 7 of *The Unsettling of America,* virtually echoes this:

  The question of human limits, of the proper definition and place of human beings within the order of Creation, finally rests upon our attitude toward our biological existence, the life of the body in this world. What value and respect do we give to our bodies? What uses do we have for them? ... What connections or responsibilities do we maintain between our bodies and the earth? These are religious questions, obviously, for our bodies are part of the Creation, and they involve us in all the issues of mystery. But the questions are also agricultural, for no matter how urban our life, our bodies live by farming; we come from the earth and return to it, and so we live in agriculture as we live in flesh. While we live, our bodies are moving particles of the earth, joined inextricably both to the soil and to the bodies of other living creatures. It is hardly surprising then, that there should be some profound resemblances between our treatment of our bodies and our treatment of the earth.[20]

Appreciation of the Earth and our relation with it is not limited to poets and religious leaders. Astronauts and those naturally innocent express it too.

ASTRONAUTS

- Sally Ride, astronaut, said:

    The view of Earth is absolutely spectacular, and the feeling of looking back and seeing your planet as a planet is just an amazing feeling. It's a totally different perspective, and it makes you appreciate, actually, how fragile our existence is. You can look at Earth's horizon and see this really, really thin royal blue line right along the horizon, and at first you don't really quite internalize what that is, and then you realize that it's Earth's atmosphere, and that that's all there is of it, and it's about as thick as the fuzz on a tennis ball, and it's everything that separates us from the vacuum of space. If we didn't have that atmosphere, we wouldn't be here, and if we do anything to destroy that atmosphere, we won't be here, so it really puts the planet in perspective.[21]

- Edgar Mitchel, astronaut, said:

    Suddenly, from behind the rim of the moon, in long, slow-motion moments of immense majesty, there emerges a sparkling blue and white jewel, a light, delicate sky-blue sphere laced with slowly swirling veils of white, rising gradually like a small pearl in a thick sea of black mystery. It takes more than a moment to fully realize this is Earth ... home.[22]

And he said:[23]

"You develop an instant global consciousness, a people orientation, an intense dissatisfaction with the state of the world, and a compulsion to do something about it. From out there on the moon, international politics look so petty. You want to grab a politician by the scruff of the neck and drag him a quarter of a million miles out and say, 'Look at that, you son of a bitch.'"

— Apollo 14 astronaut Edgar Mitchell

Figure 1.1

Mitchell's desire to awaken politicians arises from those experiences we have when the mind goes breathless, words evaporate, and our point of view explodes. We see ourselves in our actual place in the universe and stand in fresh awe of the great shower of gifts we receive. And we want everyone to stand with us.

William Anders (astronaut) later said that although the astronauts went on their mission to explore the moon, what they really discovered was the planet Earth. He added:

I think it's important for people to understand they are just going around on one of the smaller grains of sand on one of the spiral arms of this kind of puny galaxy ... it [Earth] is insignificant, but it's the only one we've got.

THE NATURALLY INNOCENT

Good night God
I hope that you are having

a good time being the world.
I like the world very much.
I'm glad you made the plants
and trees survive with the
rain and summers.
When summer is nearly near
the leaves begin to fall.
I hope you have a good time
being the world.
I like how God feels around
everyone in the world.
God, I am very happy that
I live on you.
Your arms clasp around the world.
I like you and your friends.
Every time I open my eyes
I see the gleaming sun.
I like the animals—the deer,
and us creatures of the world,
the mammals.
I love my dear friends. "
— D. B., four and a half years old.[24]

DB lives in a household that is clear about its place in the world. His is the natural gratitude available in us all. Shel Silverstein captured the Earth's spirit of offering, the source of DB's gratitude, in his book *The Giving Tree*: "Once there was a tree, and she loved a little boy."

Then she offers herself completely, bit by bit, as a place to play, as shade, as fruit, as branches, and eventually as trunk.

ENDNOTE

This First Piece considers the relationship between Earth and human-kind, a giver-receiver-gift relationship that, when deeply examined, col-lapses into itself, becoming a single piece. When A visits B with an offer, is either left untouched? Who does not give? Who does not receive? The visit itself is an equal part, and a vital role falls to B—gracious receiving.

Roshi Wendy Egyoku Nakao comments on gracious receiving in a piece in ZCLA's Water Wheel :

> ... Punna recognized that her offering fell short of a true delicacy, but it was all she had and she offered it whole-heartedly. With these words, *just as this cake, when I offered it to you, became flavorful and worthy of you,* Punna tells us that the receiver transforms the gift. Those who are concerned about giving, please be equally aware that one's receptivity is the apex of generosity.[25]

The gathering of praises and thanks in this Piece is not complete—a multitude of spirit-infused offerings have been left out. In a sense it can never be complete, for fresh thanks arise with each new breath. Robert Lax begins the introduction to *One Hundred Graces* with this:

> Grace before breathing, grace while breathing, grace after breathing ...[26]

It is just Lax's opinion that each breath should be so thanked. It is just Rilke's opinion that we accomplish God's work in the world. While some questions are best taken up in community, the question of gratitude here is personal. If life is not a gift, neither of emergence nor of Creation, then there is no need to be grateful. If we are neither evolution's nor God's agents, there is no need to serve. And without gratitude, without service, there is no need for responsibility.

SECOND PIECE

The Implications of Being Human

INTENTION

The First Piece presents that life is a gift, as if of a higher power. It reflects on the goodness of fit of human beings with the Earth and how to respond.

This Second Piece presents that humans are at the top of the intelligence chain and examines the implications of being at the top.

CLARIFYING WORDS

There are two changes in wording which may seem simple, but they represent important shifts. First, the First Piece speaks of the Earth-human relationship and the goodness of fit between Earth and humans. But this wording focuses consideration only on human beings. Deep religion recognizes that Creation is more than interwoven, it is interdependent—all plants and creatures being in relation with each other. E. O. Wilson refers to this mutually supportive relationship as "the iron law of species interdependency."[27] In Figure 2.4 we see that the human portion of Creation has grown significantly with respect to the web of life. So the Earth-human relationship now must carry the understanding that humans dominate the impact on the Earth and all its other creatures, though they are only one part of Creation, only one part of life.

Second, the word *gift*, used in the First Piece to describe what we receive from the Earth, is part of the giver-receiver-gift triad. This threesome is accompanied by baggage both as a whole and as individual pieces. The giver-receiver-gift exchange establishes social expectations that can easily end up feeling unbalanced. These expectations are honored more in the breach than in the execution, certainly when considering the gifts of the Earth.

The phrase "gifts of the earth" implies a relationship in which Earth is host/giver and humans are guest/receiver. An important aspect of this is the Earth's generosity. As Whitman says "... the earth does not withhold ... does not argue ... ". A second aspect, certainly as important as gift-not-withheld, is gift-intertwined. Each gift is not just that single item, it is the whole interdependent net that that item touches. Water, cascading from mountain snow pack, *is* the climate, weather, wildlife, river, dams, treatment plants, pipes, and faucets.

If we speak of fruits instead of gifts, we better capture this interdependence. The phrase "fruits of the earth" then refers to cyclical offerings that humans harvest, as from an orchard—an orchard which needs attentive caretaking to preserve and pass on. Robert Frost's poem "After Apple Picking" illustrates this caretaking, showing generosity, physicality, care, and economy:

- generosity (as from material left for the gleaners):

   ... and there may be two or three
   apples I didn't pick upon some bough.

- physicality:

   My instep arch not only keeps the ache,
   it also keeps the pressure of a ladder-round.

   ...

   For I have had too much
   of apple picking; I am overtired
   of the great harvest I myself desired.

- care and respect:

   There were ten thousand thousand fruit to touch,
   cherish in hand, lift down, and not let fall.

- economy:

For all
that struck the earth,
no matter if not bruised or spiked with stubble,
went surely to the cider-apple heap …[28]

Generosity, physicality, care, and economy are just some of the aspects associated naturally with fruits, less so with gifts. These aspects are saturated with conservative values. From here, these five Pieces will speak of the fruits of the earth.

GRATITUDE, SERVICE, AND RESPONSIBILITY

The First Piece introduced gratitude, service and responsibility, but more can be said about them than simple praises and thanks.

GRATITUDE

Joanna Macy, writing in a broad context, puts gratitude this way:

> The great open secret of gratitude is that it is not dependent on external circumstance. It's like a setting or channel that we can switch to at any moment, no matter what's going on around us. It helps us connect to our basic right to be here, like the breath does. It's a stance of the soul. ...
>
> Thankfulness loosens the grip of the industrial growth society by contradicting its predominant message: that we are insufficient and inadequate. The forces of late capitalism continually tell us that we need *more*—more stuff, more money, more approval, more comfort, more entertainment. The dissatisfaction it breeds is profound. ... So gratitude is liberating. ... It helps us realize that we are sufficient, and that realization frees us.[29]

Gratitude is often accompanied by a flash of emotion that rises out of comparison. If, as David Brooks has noted, a comparison results in an exceeding of expectations, the emotion is joy or delight. Brooks describes those who can be grateful even in disappointment as "grateful dispositionally".

Gratitude can be a vector such as wind, which has both magnitude and direction, or it can be a value such as temperature, which has only magnitude. Gratitude of this second kind, thankfulness in all things without need for a reason or direction (or for an ineffable reason), is described in the poem "Thanks" by W. S. Merwin:

Listen
with the night falling we are saying thank you
we are stopping on the bridge to bow from the railings
we are running out of the glass rooms
with our mouths full of food to look at the sky
and say thank you
we are standing by the water looking out
in different directions
back from a series of hospitals back from a mugging
after funerals we are saying thank you
after the news of the dead
whether or not we knew them we are saying thank you
in a culture up to its chin in shame
living in the stench it has chosen we are saying thank you
over telephones we are saying thank you
in doorways and in the backs of cars and in elevators
remembering wars and the police at the back door
and the beatings on stairs we are saying thank you
in the banks that use us we are saying thank you
with the crooks in office with the rich and fashionable
unchanged we go on saying thank you thank you
with the animals dying around us
our lost feelings we are saying thank you
with the forests falling faster than the minutes
of our lives we are saying thank you
with the words going out like the cells of a brain
with the cities growing over us like the earth
we are saying thank you faster and faster
with nobody listening we are saying thank you
we are saying thank you and waving

dark though it is[30]

Merwin is writing of the dispositionally grateful,[31] those who can even be thankful for a disappointment when it yields a useful lesson.

Sallie Jiko Tisdale points out that the feeling of thankfulness is both simple and profound, and when we are glad for what we have we can be generous.

> Gratitude, the simple and profound feeling of being thankful, is the foundation of all generosity. I am generous when I believe that right now, right here, in this form and place, I am myself being given what I need. Generosity requires that we relinquish something, and this is impossible if we are not glad for what we have. Otherwise the giving hand closes into a fist and won't let go.[32]

SERVICE

Gratitude often elicits an impulse to respond. When that impulse flows freely, the transition from gratitude to service is as natural as saying thank you, and serving just emerges. The impulse is to share both the gift and the thankfulness. Serving does this. Serving is the glue holding best friends together. It's the teamwork in an Army squad, a soup kitchen, an emergency room.

Like many things, serving exists on a spectrum. For some it means action; for some, just to be is to serve. Service, whether it's an ongoing process or an ad hoc task, whether it receives thanks and recognition or not, satisfies.

In addition to rising out of gratitude, service can also rise from the acknowledgment of need. In this case, service unites giver, receiver, and gift, bringing personal intimacy to the situation. The gift is often not an object, not something manufactured, but an offering of time and self. In a blog post David Brooks writes

> We live in a capitalist meritocracy that encourages individualism and utilitarianism, ambition and pride. But this society would fall apart if not for another economy,

one in which gifts surpass expectations, in which insuf-
ficiency is acknowledged and dependence celebrated.[33,34]
Service comprises these gifts, supporting us and linking us together.
Rilke, recognizing himself as servant, writes:

> What will you do, God, when I die?
> I am your pitcher (when I shatter?)
> I am your drink (when I go bitter?)
> I, your garment; I, your craft.
> Without me, what reason have you?
> Without me what house
> where intimate words await you?
> I, velvet sandal that falls from your foot.
> I, cloak dropping from your shoulder.
> Your gaze, which I welcome now
> as it warms my cheek,
> will search for me hour after hour
> and lie at sunset, spent,
> on an empty beach
> among unfamiliar stones.
> What will you do, God? I am afraid.[35]

RESPONSIBILITY

Serving fulfills responsibility, so the question becomes responsibility to who or for what? One can take responsibility for the past, but the
responsibility of service points to the present and thus the future.

Dennis Potter, English TV dramatist, said:

> The nowness of everything is absolutely wonderful. [...] If
> you see the present tense, boy do you see it, and boy can
> you celebrate it.[36]

Now is currently a popular orientation, but it must be acknowledged
that now is not consequence free, it is directly responsible for the future.
One cannot live in now and be free from the consequences of one's actions.
Standing upright in now, aware of both one's freedom of action and one's
impact on the future, is called responsibility.

Sallie McFague, in *The Body Of God*, says

> Our loyalty needs to move beyond family, nation, and
> even our own species to identify, in the broadest possible
> horizon, with all life: we *are* citizens of planet earth.
>
> Such identification is not sentimental. ... It is simply the
> truth about who we are ... We are profoundly interrelated
> and interdependent with everything living and nonliv-
> ing in the universe and especially on our planet, and our
> peculiar position here is that we are radically dependent
> on all that is, so to speak, "beneath" us ... . At the same
> time we have become, like it or not, the guardians and
> caretakers of our tiny planet. ... We are the responsible
> ones, responsible for all the rest upon which we are so
> profoundly dependent.[37]

The poet Anne Porter has written movingly about responsibility in
her poem *A Short Testament*, only asking God's help when she is unable
to first set things right herself. Her plea is the heart of both atonement
and responsibility.

> A Short Testament
> Whatever harm I may have done
> in all my life in all your wide creation
> if I cannot repair it
> I beg you to repair it,
> And then there are all the wounded
> the poor the deaf the lonely and the old
> whom I have roughly dismissed
> as if I were not one of them.
> Where I have wronged them by it
> and cannot make amends
> I ask you
> to comfort them to overflowing,
> And where there are lives I may have withered
> around me,
> or lives of strangers far or near
> that I've destroyed in blind complicity,

and if I cannot find them
or have no way to serve them,
remember them. I beg you to remember them
when winter is over
and all your unimaginable promises
burst into song on death's bare branches.[38]

Gratitude, service, responsibility—these are the important understandings about our place on the Earth, whether they've been acquired through evolution or Creation, through thoughtfulness or through Genesis 2:15.[39] They are the implications of being human.

THE TOP OF THE INTELLIGENCE CHAIN

Because we can't communicate well with other species and because we have only recently come to appreciate the various categories of our own intelligence,[40] it may be a while before we can truly claim that our form(s) of intelligence surpass all others. Nevertheless, we believe that certain physical abilities (such as mobility, communication, manual dexterity), in combination with mental abilities (such as accumulation of knowledge, development of tools and processes, self-awareness) put us at the top of the intelligence chain.

Or maybe it was chance that put us here. Evolution and geology say that our ancient forbearers were way down the food chain and at the mercy of dinosaurs and other carnivores when a meteor changed everything.

Eons later, on the savanna, our mobility was not sufficient to escape predators but it let us move upright on the part of the Earth that is solid, imposing the need to deal with gravity and verticality and bringing awareness of the stars. Though communication is fragmented by thousands of languages, it is intricate enough in each to represent and transmit subtle concepts. Our manual dexterity, though modest, supports Mozart, prestidigitation, and brain surgery. Our knowledge is stored in major libraries of every kind in every country; it's saved in the Svalbard Global Seed Vault and in the Cloud. We have tools that can manipulate single atoms and processes which erect the Burj Khalifa towers. We can see into the human body and out to the origins of the universe. And we claim self-awareness, which enables awe and wonder and teaches us of our vulnerability to entitlement, hubris, impatience, and narrow vision.

This ability to understand and manipulate the physical world has enabled us to grow to our present numbers and attain dominion over the Earth. The flip side of this capacity is responsibility. Accomplished warriors, knowing of power and its effects, develop wisdom and restraint. Such warriors understand the importance of walking softly, easily, of listening.

HUMANITY'S SIZE

The implications of being at the top of the intelligence chain include considerations of humanity's size, scope, and stature. These have direct bearing on what we are called to do and our degree of responsibility.

A couple of centuries ago, the Earth could keep up with human consumption and waste. Before the mid-1700s the Earth's population was less than a billion, lived mostly rurally, was powered by animals, and its technology was based primarily on renewables like water wheels, windmills, weights, escapements, and springs.

This changed with the agricultural and industrial revolutions. Ruth DeFries, focusing on the ratchets and pivots in the search for sufficient food, writes of the Norfolk four-course system of crop rotation that emerged in the mid-18th century:

> … The impact was so colossal that the period is termed the agricultural revolution.
>
> The result of the revolution was a surplus of food. Whether the surplus spurred England's industrial revolution of the eighteenth century or the other way around is impossible to say. … But there's no doubt that surplus food was available to feed the growing cities and the human laborers who worked the machines of the textile mills and other factories. The growing industries meant greater demand for the surplus food, which in turn created incentives for farmers to produce more. …[41]

Everything came together to empower population growth, though Thomas Robert Malthus saw it differently. By the turn of the century (1798) he had published his article "An Essay on the Principle of Population".

> Malthus, a political economist, argued that humans were destined to grow geometrically, while food production could increase only arithmetically, guaranteeing that famine would cinch the growth of humankind within the scarce purse of resources.

> And so it did. For 150 years after Malthus, hunger killed millions: perhaps 50 million Chinese in multiple famines of the 19th century; upwards of 20 million Indians during a dozen major famines in the latter half of the 19th century; a million in the Great Famine of Ireland between 1845 and 1852; one-third of the local population in the Ethiopian Great Famine of 1888 to 1892; 3 million in Bengal in 1943.[42]

These famines continue today in the Middle East, in parts of Africa, and around the world. That some of these people died from maldistribution and poverty does not reduce the suffering and waste.

Figure 2.1 shows birth rate, death rate, and population curves plotted over about the last three centuries. This idealized interpretation is called the demographic transition. It offers an academic attempt to explain the relationship between the three curves in stages—high stationary, early expanding, late expanding, low stationary, and declining?[43] The concept of demographic transition is discussed in Joel Cohen's book *How Many People Can the Earth Support?*[44]

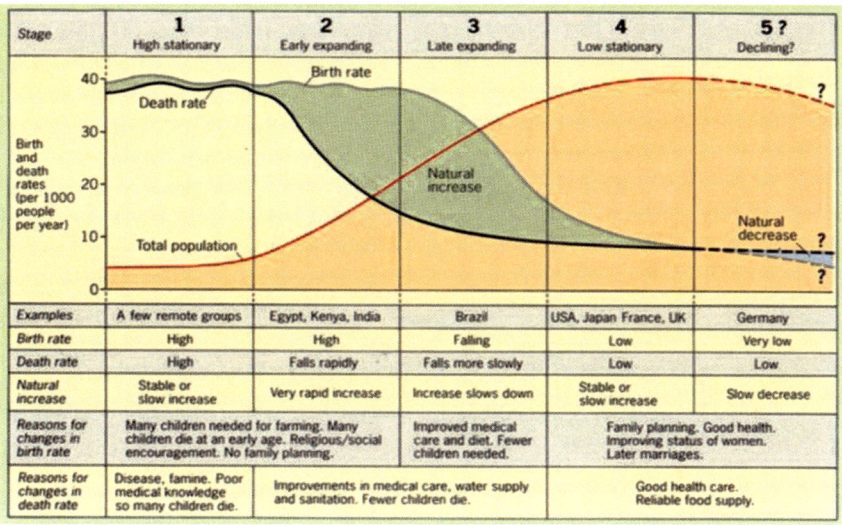

Figure 2.1

This is an idealized graph as can be seen by comparing it with Figure 2.4. Figure 2.4, using actual world data, shows no hint of the flattening and cresting of late Stage 3 and Stage 4. Instead, it shows a shape like early Stage 3, with population still in a vigorous climb. And even if the whole world were to suddenly acquire a below-replacement birth rate, the population would continue to increase as the babies born in the previous 20 to 30 years come into childbearing age.

Although Figure 2.1 is an intellectual explanation of what could or might happen, it's instructive to put dates on it. They might well go like this:

- The left boundary of Stage 1, high stationary, is arbitrary at 1700 CE. Had that left boundary been drawn at 5,000 BCE, the birth rate, death rate, and population curves between then and 1700 would have been much the same as Stage 1—high stationary.

- The boundary between Stages 1 and 2, where the death rate begins to drop, is often placed in the mid-1700s, about the time of the agricultural and industrial revolutions referenced by Ruth DeFries.

John Trotter

- The boundary between Stages 2 and 3, where the birth rate begins to drop, is vague. Another, similar graph for the United Kingdom places that point at about 1880.

- The boundary between Stages 3 and 4 is placed on that same UK graph at about 1930 to 1940.

- The boundary between Stages 4 and 5 is up for grabs. Those countries that triggered the alarm that Pat Buchanan sounded in *The Death of the West* are indeed showing below-replacement fertility rates, but the Earth as a whole is still growing. In fact, the Earth's population curve so far shows none of the flattening of the idealized low stationary stage of Figure 2.1.

Typical population pyramids for countries have been constructed for four stages in a population's evolution, as shown in Figure 2.2.[45]

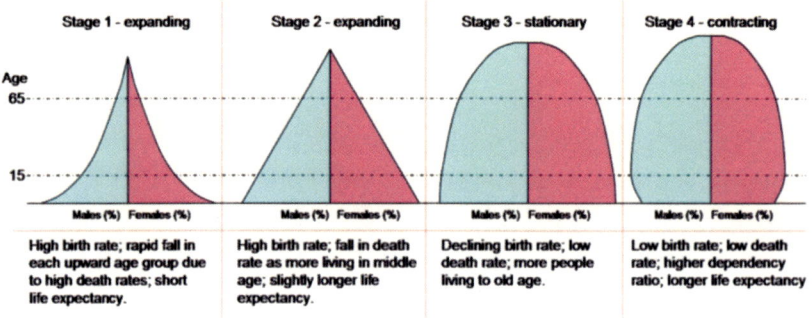

Figure 2.2

A real-life pyramid showing expansion, as in Stage 1 of Figure 2.2 is seen in Nigeria's 2015 population pyramid (shown in Figure 2.3a).[46] It shows a high population of children who, as the country's death rate drops, will change the pyramid into a shape like Stage 2 above.

28

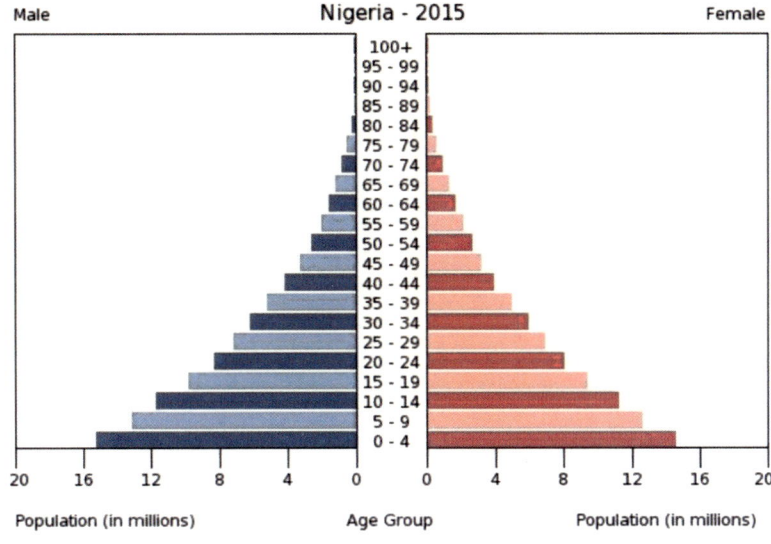

Figure 2.3a

A real-life pyramid showing contraction as in Stage 4 of Figure 2.2 is seen in Japan's 2015 population pyramid (shown in Figure 2.3b).[47] Note that unless a constantly shrinking population is assumed, this is a transient situation. In a single generation or so, this curve will look more and more like a full-bodied (though narrower) Stage 3 of Figure 2.2 as the smaller generation moves up in age.

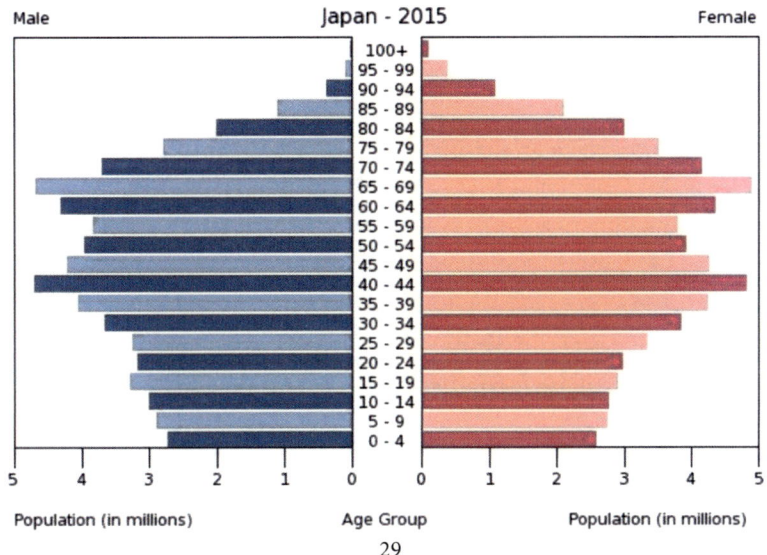

Figure 2.3b

When population is plotted over a wider time span than is used for Figure 2.1, the green area of Figure 2.1 (natural increase) gives one a sense of human population's recent dramatic rise:[48]

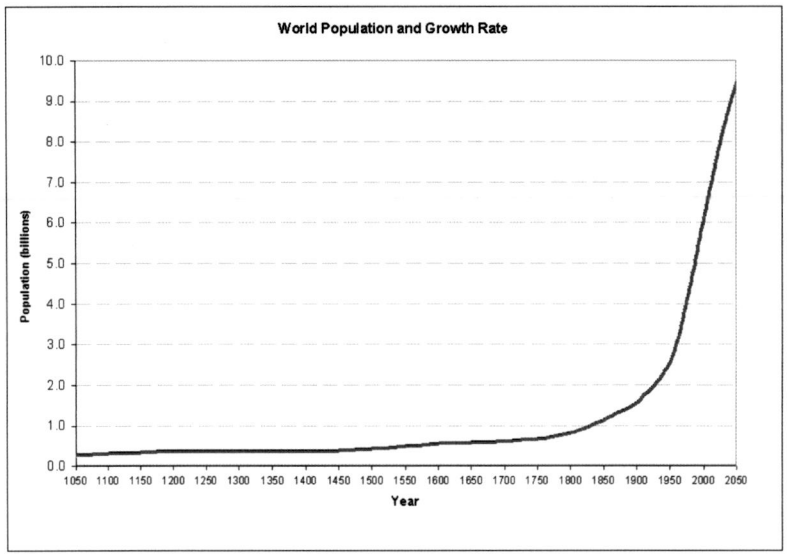

Figure 2.4[49]

This curve, called a 'J' curve, is unique in the history of human beings, but not in nature. If this curve represented bacterial counts in a baby, it would cause despair. If it represented fruit flies in an experiment jar, we know how it ends. The curve shows an estimated population of about 9.4 billion in 2050, only 35 years from now (more or less a generation). From a historical perspective, our numbers dwarf any previous period. The curve appears like it could be, for the Earth as a whole, Stages 2 and 3 of Figure 2.1, the only difference being horizontal scale.

Given the great variation in each country's current fertility rates, it's impossible to say how far along the Earth is in Stage 3 of the demographic transition. And given the various cultural attitudes toward fertility, it's not possible to predict when the Earth as a whole may drop its birth rate to match its death rate.

A curve similar to Figure 2.4 is presented in Mark Bush's *Ecology of a Changing Planet*. He suggests three possible outcomes:

- Population will continue to increase exponentially until a biological carrying capacity is reached. This is unlikely to happen because we will work to limit population before then.

- Population will grow to an asymptote that is lower than the biological carrying capacity, and it will stabilize there. Predicted sizes for such a population, based on resource availability, vary from 11 to 16 billion people, that upper number more than twice the current population.

- Population will continue to grow until it reaches a threshold at which famine, disease, and warfare cause a decline. One influential prediction advanced by the Club of Rome suggested a slump of population in the twenty-second century that would prune our numbers back to about 6 billion.[50]

The slump mentioned in Bush's third point represents enormous suffering, since about half of the Earth's population would die prematurely from famine, disease, and war. Thirty-five years ago Carlo Cipolla wrote that

> The looser the adjustment of the birth rate to the death rate the higher the probability of ... peaks [in the death rate]. If we breed like rabbits, in the long run we have to die like rabbits.[51]

What can be said about the reaction of a complex system like the Earth to a spike of population such as we've had in the last 250 years? The Earth itself is giving one answer with the environmental issues laid out later in the Third Piece: it's building up CO_2 to record levels in the air and oceans, and suffering the toxic effects of modern pollution. Humans are giving opposing reactions. One is to predict crises due to overconsumption and pollution. The other is to deny a problem, declare the increased resourcefulness of the larger population an opportunity, or change the topic to economics. Ruth DeFries notes in *The Big Ratchet*, that:

> From the multimillennia lens ... two themes emerge. One is that the ratchets, hatchets, and pivots will continue as long as human civilization exists. Solutions will

create new problems, and problems will generate new solutions.[52]

Sad news indeed, because even if only a single new problem rises out of each solution, no real progress has been made.

Then, too, the cyclic nature of ratchets-hatchets-pivots means that though we are now in a ratchet, a period of (maldistributed, poverty-limited) food surplus, we are headed for a hatchet, a period of scarcity and desperation.

HUMANITY'S SCOPE

Humanity's scope is related to size (count) in that as numbers rise, space that was previously open and wild, and available to other species, comes under human influence. The same increase in population that crowds other life out of its habitat also makes a more crowded world for each human being. This matters, because for the Earth and all its creatures this crowding is ongoing and cumulative, while for the individual it lurks as stress and defensiveness.

Wendell Berry speaks about the relationship of humans to the Earth in his essay *The Body and The Earth*. Here he speaks of size not as a number, but as physical scale:

> That humans are small within the Creation is an ancient perception, represented often enough in art that it must be supposed to have an elemental importance. On one of the painted walls of the Lascaux cave (20,000–15,000 BCE), surrounded by the exquisitely shaped, shaded, and colored bodies of animals, there is the childish stick figure of a man, a huntsman who, having cast his spear into the guts of a bison, is now weaponless and vulnerable, poignantly frail, exposed, and incomplete. The message seems essentially that of the voice out of the whirlwind in the Book of Job: the Creation is bounteous and mysterious, and humanity is only a part of it—not its equal, much less its master.

Old Chinese landscape paintings reveal, among tower-
ing mountains, the frail outline of a roof or a tiny human
figure passing along a road on foot or horseback. These
landscapes are almost always populated. ... What is represented is a world in which humans belong, but which
does not belong to humans in any tidy economic sense;
the Creation provides a place for humans, but it is greater
than humanity and within it even great men are small.
Such humility is the consequence of an accurate insight,
ecological in its bearing, not a pious deference to 'spiritual' value.[53]

Though each individual person is small and has little impact, collectively humans now saturate and dominate the Earth. Humanity's scope,
now little different from the point of view of the artists who painted the
cave walls or the Chinese landscapes, is truly global. Google Earth shows
us everywhere; satellites measure continental drift and the earliest stages
of the universe; communication is omnipresent and brings news from the
10 directions.

I formed the basis for my long-term point of view, my sense of open
space, my sense of what a big city is, and my sense of privacy in the late
1940s, when there were a third as many people as there are now. These
impressions remain in me as unquestioned baselines. My son formed his
baselines in the mid-1970s, and his son in the first decade of the 2000s.
The world now feels very crowded and intrusive to me, but normal to my
grandson. If the population curve had been flat through those years, there
would be little difference in our baselines, but it looked like Figure 2.4 so
my son, and grandson, and each generation born during a sharply rising
population curve will understand population density and city size and privacy differently because of this continuous shift of reference.

Scope is more than just a matter of geographic presence, it also has an
economic aspect. We have organized ourselves culturally by tribal, local,
regional, national, and multinational points of view. We have experienced
hunter-gathering, agricultural, industrial, and technological points of
view. And we freely use each of these different points of view at different
times. But both the cultural and the economic points of view are unevenly

distributed geographically, with some regions still operating from almost every perspective. Furthermore, given the degree of population growth, the extent of international trade, the global impact of environmental concerns, and the speed and reach of media and communication, a new point of view—a global scope—is calling to be added to the mix. This will have both a cultural and an economic impact until we can freely think from and use this global point of view.

Over 35 years ago Carlo Cipolla pointed out the disturbing impact of the transition from one economic organization to another.[54] Parts of the developed world are dealing with industrial to technological transitions, while other parts of the world are dealing with farming to industrial transitions combined with tribal to national transitions. Not only these transitions, but the disparities between developed and developing worlds, contribute directly to social unrest.

Similar such disruptions are certain to accompany the change to a global scope, since such a shift can threaten the identity and potentially the existence of any group that doesn't see global scope as essential. The shift may also rebound to threaten any group that tries to impose or hurry it. Carlo Cipolla wrote:

> The introduction of modern techniques in environments
> that are still dominated by intolerance and aggressiveness
> is a most alarming development. ... Instructing a savage
> in advanced techniques does not change him into a civi-
> lized person; it just makes him an efficient savage.[55]

It's currently a time of global unemployment and unrest. A shift to a global point-of-view will be slow, difficult, painful, and unfair, no matter how essential it is.

HUMANITY'S STATURE

At least three major dictionaries begin their definitions of stature with height.[56] But here stature has less to do with height than with depth. Stature is a complex variable. Being a complex variable means that a person may have stature with regard to honesty, but not thrift, or stature with regard to creativity, but not relationships. Similarly, a nation may have stature with regard to military strength, but not with regard to the environment. Stature is subjective and depends on the views of others, and becomes generally accepted only through the agreement of many like-minded peers.

Since stature is most often seen as a quality of persons, what does humanity's stature mean? A person's stature is expressed in his or her actions and assessed by peers. Similarly, a nation's stature is expressed in its actions and assessed both by its peers and by people. Humanity doesn't have peers as such, so we could say humanity's stature is expressed in humankind's global actions and may be assessed by those people and nations who themselves have stature in the quality being assessed. Such assessments are not snapshots, rather they are ongoing evaluations, their important features being their trend and their constancy.

Humanity's stature is not dependent on population size—more, or fewer, people do not directly affect stature. The dictionaries mentioned above go on to mention degree of development, intellectual or moral greatness, esteem or status based on one's positive qualities or achievements, and one who has earned high regard. The qualities assessed many things such as how differences are resolved, how the young and the old are treated, and the breadth and depth of those qualities.

So the work is to develop humanity's stature from a whole-Earth view such that humanity can be said to have an admirable stature in all its qualities. That means people and nations living in partnership with all life and with respect for the Earth—something Native Americans, for instance, understand and do naturally.

THE EARTH'S POINT OF VIEW

Holding in mind the size and scope of humans shown in Figure 2.4, consider again the old Chinese landscapes that Wendell Berry refers to. The artists have worked from a point of view and a scope wider than that of a single individual. They have opened up their worldview to see from a grand perspective. One could argue that their stature exceeds their scale. Just the size of our current population means that this grander point of view, this global point of view, must now be included and acknowledged alongside our individual, family, community, and national points of view.

In some ways, a global point of view is emerging on its own. The news is global now and full of world concerns about international trade partnerships, terrorism, defense alliances, and flows of resources, ideas, refugees, humanitarian aid, food, medicine, and waste. This news arrives not just through the mainstream media but through the intimacy of our personal phones and tablets and social circles. It brings with it a shift toward global awareness that is full of contradictions—defense alliances and global terrorism bind us into defensive clusters, while recovery from war or natural disaster reminds us that we are all in this together.

WHO HOLDS THE EARTH'S POINT OF VIEW?

The question of who looks out for the Earth would not even come up if we were attacked by space-aliens. All peoples of the Earth would unite and face the threat with a single roar. But such external threats are rare. What will it take to unify the Earth into a community that cares for itself as a grandmother cares for her household?

To hold the Earth's point of view is to understand that:
- this one Earth is all we have,
- all life interdepends, to say *we* is to mean all peoples, all creatures, all life,
- all economic activity rests in and on the health of the Earth:
    We easily forget that the economic structure which man
    has erected rests entirely on the Earth's natural resources
    and processes. Economic activity depends on the Earth's
    capacity to supply raw materials, to produce food, and to
    absorb waste. Without these factors, there would be not
    even the most rudimentary economic activities on which
    man's existence depends.[57]

Who has the right to speak for the Earth? Many say that God has given Creation into our stewardship. Others say that evolution has delivered Earth into our stewardship. Either way, humans appear to be responsible, at least until we can communicate with other species and obtain access to their experience, insight, and wisdom. Consequently, it becomes important to keep records of the Earth, her measures and populations; to know her natural rhythms and balances, ebbs and flows, blooms and decays; her capacities for cleansing and regeneration. Then, if the natural rhythms and balances must be disturbed, we can plan for the consequences.

Who holds the Earth's point of view?

- *The Green Bible* points to Genesis 2:15, in which Adam and his descendants are put in the garden with a purpose—to till it and keep it.

- Native Americans hold the Earth with deep respect:

    Treat the earth and all of her aspects as your mother. Show deep respect for the mineral world, the plant world, and the animal world. Do nothing to pollute the air or the soil. If others want to destroy our mother, rise up with wisdom to defend her.[58]

- Zen master John Daido Loori says:

    It is no small thing to be born human. With it comes a tremendous responsibility. That responsibility is due to our intelligence, our awareness. We have the power, each of us, not only to change our own lives and bring them into harmony with the ten thousand things, but also to nourish others, to heal this planet.[59]

- In *A Timbered Choir* Wendell Berry offers:

    ...
    We join our work to Heaven's gift,
    our hope to what is left,
    that field and woods at last agree
    in an economy
    of widest worth.
    High Heaven's Kingdom come on earth.
    ... [60]

ENDNOTE

Ruth DeFries writes

    To comprehend how our species—which for tens of thousands of years hunted prey and gathered wild plants like any other animal—became such a dominant force demands that we leave behind narrow-minded moralizing about conquest or destruction. A broader perspective views human civilization as neither right nor wrong, neither good nor bad, but as part of the evolution of life on this planet.[61]

While true in the absolute sense, this perspective is not appropriate when choosing what to do in the world. It dismisses gratitude for the Earth's fruits and for human strengths. It is bereft of service and responsibility for the future, and as devoid of compassion and morality as Nature itself.

More appropriate is Rilke, who expressed dedication and gratitude so well in the First Piece. Here he looks to the future and speaks of cycles and rhythms, and, ultimately, our purpose:

> All will come again into its strength:
> the fields undivided, the waters undammed,
> the trees towering and the walls built low,
> and in the valleys, people as strong
> and varied as the land.
> And no churches where God
> is imprisoned and lamented
> like a trapped and wounded animal.
> The houses welcoming all who knock
> and a sense of boundless offering
> in all relations, and in you and me.
> No yearning for an afterlife, no looking beyond,
> no belittling of death,
> but only longing for what belongs to us
> and serving earth, lest we remain unused.[62]

We find ourselves showered by the uncomplaining generosity of the Earth. When we step out of the way, the natural response that rises from our depths is gratitude, thankfulness. From this and from awareness of the issues facing the Earth, we serve because we can see the results of failure to serve. We have the tools to correct the problems—our hands and our minds. Whether we work as God's agents or simply as those who have acquired a bit of knowledge and control, when we look out on Creation from the Earth's point of view we see that we, at the top of the intelligence chain, are the ultimate stewards of the Earth.

THIRD PIECE

A Survey of Issues and Discovery of a Common Factor

If you repeat it enough, even politicians can come to understand the root.

INTENTION

The First Piece presents that life is a gift, as if of a higher power. It reflects on the goodness of fit of human beings with the Earth and how to respond.

The Second Piece presents that humans are at the top of the intelligence chain and examines the implications of being at the top.

This Third Piece inventories many of the current environmental issues afflicting the Earth. It finds population to be a factor common to each issue.

BACKGROUND

Before looking into the Earth's issues, it's useful to address the question of our relationship with and our use of the Earth. Decades ago, in his book *The Unsettling of America,* Wendell Berry commented on agriculture and our cultural evolution:

> We can understand a great deal of our history ... by thinking of ourselves as divided into conquerors and victims. In order to understand our own time and predicament ... we would do well to shift the terms and say that we are divided between exploitation and nurture. ... Whereas the exploiter asks of a piece of land only how much and how quickly it can be made to produce, the nurturer asks

a question that is much more complex and difficult: What is its carrying capacity?[63]

Berry uses the terms *exploiter* and *nurturer* because we all have both qualities, which is less true of the terms *conqueror* and *victim*. When we adopt the role of exploiter, we set aside our ideals, we no longer honor the past with our gratitude, and we discredit concern for the future and the consequences of our actions. When we adopt the role of nurturer, we offer thanksgiving, service, and responsibility. Nurturing honors that which brought us here and carries us whole into the future.

One of the characteristics of recent manufacturing abilities is that they can create new things more economically than used ones can be repaired. This was a predictable consequence of the combination of miniaturization with mass production and low wages which was not well thought through. It has led to a throwaway behavior directly counter to responsibility to the future. This gives some evidence about the nature of a culture—it can be called exploitive to the extent that it does not plan for its discards. Planning for discards involves more than just finding a dumping place.

> When one acquires something, he or she assumes responsibility for it. As they use and enjoy it they continue that responsibility. That care does not end until the thing has been disposed of with an attentive mind.
>
> Or, if one accepts responsibility for something not his or her own (borrows or caretakes or leases something), they do so as if they had bought it themselves and for a dear price, and they care for it and return it whole.
>
> But this is not news. So, trusting your own sense of value and triage, note that there are systems in place to recycle both things with residual value and those without, and that recycling begins with attentive creation and acquisition.[64]

And note that attentive acquisition includes using common sense and a long-term view to see through marketing hype and peer pressure.

ENVIRONMENTAL ISSUES

The Second Piece ended with the conclusion that we humans are at the top of the intelligence chain and are the ultimate stewards of the Earth. A first task, then, is to assess the state of the Earth that we are to protect and serve.

If you check Wikipedia for 'list of environmental issues' you are taken to a page with 31 major headings.[65] Each of these major headings themselves contain from 2 entries (Ozone depletion) to 24 entries (Toxicants). Alan Weisman, on p409 of his book *Countdown*, writes of a paper published in the journal *Nature* with versions in *Ecology and Society* and *Scientific American*. It lists nine boundaries important to sustainability. All nine of these boundaries are found in the Wikipedia list, and the two lists can be matched up this way:

Nature boundaries	Wikipedia issues
climate change	climate change
biodiversity loss	biodiversity, habitat destruction (under Ecosystems, Land use); by-catch (under Fishing); clear-cutting (under Forest); species extinction (under Species)
disruption of global phosphorus and nitrogen cycles	eutrophication (under Environmental degradation and Water pollution); nutrient pollution (under Intensive farming)
ozone depletion	ozone depletion
ocean acidification	ocean acidification (under Climate change and Water pollution)

freshwater use	water crisis (under Water depletion and Water pollution)
changes in land use	Land use, Sea-level* rise (under Climate change); Habitat destruction (under Ecosystems, Environmental degradation, Species); Scorched earth (under Environmental issues with war); Clear-cutting, Deforestation (under Forests); Slash and burn (under Intensive farming); Mountaintop removal mining (under Mining); Soil erosion, Soil contamination, Soil salinization (under Soil); Invasive species (under Species); Landfill (under Waste)
chemical pollution	Toxicants, Volatile organic compounds (under Air pollution); Endocrine disruptors (under Environmental health); Agent orange (under Environmental issues with war); Cyanide fishing (under Fishing); Nutrient pollution, Pesticide drift (under Intensive farming); Acid mine drainage, Slurry impoundments (under Mining); Superfund sites (under Soil); Mercury in fish (under pollution)

atmospheric particulates	Atmospheric particulate matter, Environmental impact of the coal industry (under Air pollution)

*See note[66]

Note that virtually none of these were issues as few as 200 to 250 years ago. They have come into being right alongside the rising population of the last two and a half centuries. Note, too, that many of these issues impact the basic levels of Maslow's hierarchy of needs—Physiological (air, water, food, clothing, shelter) and Safety (personal safety, financial security, health, and well-being).

We can bring together these two lists and combine them still further with other lists, such as the one suggested by the chapter titles in Lester Brown, Gary Gardner, and Brian Halweil's book *Beyond Malthus*. Copyrighted in 1999 by the Worldwatch Institute, it updates an earlier paper and presents 19 dimensions of the population challenge with chapter titles like Fresh Water, Biodiversity, Cropland, Climate Change, and Waste. Combining these lists does not bring the issues into sharper focus, but it does indicate that different authors and different approaches agree on which issues are important.

Two issues, one current and the other in the near future, illustrate the centrality of all these related topics. The current issue is clean water, the near future's issue is nuclear waste.

> About four billion people, or two-thirds of the world's population, face severe water shortages during at least one month every year, far more than was previously thought, according to Arjen Y. Hoekstra, a professor of water management at the University of Twente in the Netherlands.
>
> An area experiences severe water scarcity when its farms, industries and households consume double the amount of water available in that area.

> That means that groundwater levels are falling, lakes are drying up, less water is flowing in rivers, and water supplies for industry and farmers are threatened...[67]

Nuclear radiation is the issue for the near future, not only from nuclear accidents but from uranium mine tailings, the contaminated land and water they produce, and the as yet unsolved long-term storage of radioactive wastes.[68,69,70] Complicating the issue is how climate disruption will affect secure storage. A stable, predictable climate is important in the selection of storage places for radioactive waste, but may be hard to find and guarantee in the future. The effects of the generation of greenhouse gases (climate commotion) appear only after a time delay, making such selection very difficult.

Nearly 30 years after the Chernobyl disaster, mixed results are being reported from the effects of radiation in the exclusion zone. This unnatural selection brought biodiversity in the zone down by about 50 percent, but some species of birds seem to be adapting to the increased radiation by producing higher levels of antioxidants.[71] The estimated safe reentry time for humans to the reactor area is 20,000 years.[72] As this is written, a huge steel shield, hundreds of meters in size, has been slid over the disaster site.[73] In 2011, Chernobyl was officially declared a tourist attraction.

Seventy years after the United States conducted atomic-bomb tests on Bikini Atoll, the results are mixed.

> When the United States government persuaded residents of Bikini Atoll in the Marshall Islands to leave their homes, they were told they'd be able to return as soon as the nuclear tests were over.
>
> Seventy years have passed since those promises, and the chain of islands remain deserted. Although residents are desperate to return, it appears the time has not yet come for the long-anticipated homecoming. ...
>
> While Enewetak and Rongelap appeared to have "safe" levels of gamma ray emissions, the radiation measurements did not consider other exposure pathways—for example, possible contamination of the food that local residents were eating. In the 1970s, for instance, it was

discovered that cesium 137 had contaminated the food chain on Bikini Atoll. That's how the dangerous isotope had found its way into the bodies of the islanders who'd moved back there.

As such, the researchers said they were not able to make a determination as to whether these islands were safe for habitation.

…

UNESCO has declared Bikini Atoll to be a World Heritage Site, a reminder of the lingering impacts of the Cold War and the nuclear arms race.[74]

Neil deGrasse Tyson offers a big-picture view that challenges our sense of responsibility:

Earth will be here regardless of what we do. It's whether we are wise enough to be shepherds of our own future.[75]

We're left to conclude that environmental issues are many, and understanding them and appreciating their impact involves examining them deeply. When we do that, we see how interlinked they are with each other and with life itself.

All of these boundaries and issues involve the biosphere, that tender layer of air, water and soil that supports life. It is, at most, only 14 miles thick. Astronaut Sally Ride has compared it to the fuzz on a tennis ball, but even that seems thick as a description. The biosphere may be better described as an onion skin when compared to the 4,000-mile radius of the Earth. Carlo Cipolla comments on the fragility of the biosphere early in his book *The Economic History of World Population.*[76]

Figure 3.1

Earth from space, with moon

From the viewpoint of our separate selves, the Earth is enormous and we may despair of our ability to address its issues. But Joanna Macy writes in *Active Hope* of coming to a wider sense of self. She describes circles of connection (and thus of rootedness) moving outward from individual, to family, to partner, to community, to nation, to world. She writes:

> When we identify with something larger than ourselves, whether that be our family, a circle of friends, a team, or a community, that becomes part of who we are. There is so much more to us than just a separate self; our connected self is based on recognizing that we are part of many larger circles.
>
> In the course of a day we move between these different expressions of identity. … If we feel a sense of belonging when viewing a photo of earth from space, that reflects the planetary dimension of our connected self. Our sense of rootedness comes from experiencing these more encompassing circles of our identity.[77]

A COMMON FACTOR

A common factor for all these issues lies within this biosphere. In *Countdown*, Alan Weisman, speaking of scientists and their boundaries, identifies it this way:

> Behind each of these [boundaries] was the same unspoken cause: cumulative human presence, for which they did not hazard a boundary. A decision to limit one's own species is so emotionally loaded that the very idea is as troubling to scientists as it is to any human.[78]

That last sentence can be read as insulting to scientists, but it simply makes the point that discussing cumulative human presence raises existential fears. A decision to limit one's own species is emotionally loaded and troubling, but it's not unheard of—the Fourth Piece delves into this complex and sensitive subject, considering a wide variety of conditions and situations that look directly into the face of such sacrifice.

We shy away from discussion of population size reflexively. Yet we freely manage animal populations, breeding them for food, for experimentation, and for show.[79,80] And we control populations of fish and game, licensing their killing for sport[81] and protecting, even manipulating, their existence for genetic diversity. The history of humans is dark with infanticide and with the genocidal violence of one culture over another. All this despite the interconnected, codependent relationship between the Earth and its life.

In a *New York Times* article, Eduardo Porter wrote

> There is a strong case to be made that the world faces sustainability issues whether it has nine billion people, seven billion people or four billion people," said John Wilmoth, who directs the United Nations Population Division. "Nobody can deny that population growth is a major driving factor, but in terms of the policy response, what are you going to do?[82]

How sad. Wilmoth, and so many others, seem to be unaware that Worldwatch.org has nine clear, voluntary policies to reduce population growth.[83]

Environmental issues are complex. That fewer people are important to sustainability is, of course, only an opinion—not everyone agrees that the Earth is imperiled by too many people. Julian Simon presents a vigorous objection to this idea in his books and writings.[84] Pat Buchanan is alarmed at the below-replacement birth rates in many European countries,[85] P. J. O'Rourke writes humorously about overpopulation in *All the Trouble in the World*,[86] and David Biello writes

> ... that humans, on the whole, have never been better off—whether the metric be population, wealth or some other measure. Any ecological degradation has not led to a collapse in human welfare.[87]

The key phrase in Biello's statement is "on the whole". It shifts the focus away from the individual to the general, about which all kinds of assertions can be made, while it's the individual who suffers.

A MATTER OF (HORIZONTAL) SCALE

Lest Figure 2.4 in the Second Piece give the wrong impression, lest its smooth and graceful shape fail to raise alarm, here is that same data re-plotted three times at three different horizontal scales.[88]

First, in Figure 3.2 the horizontal scale is zoomed in from Cohen's 1,000,000 BC to encompass the majority (according to anthropologists) of human history. The starting year of 300,000 BC is a number smaller than Cohen's, but one that would allow showing both the approximate times of anatomically modern humans and the Creation event.[89] The vertical scale is set to show the current population.

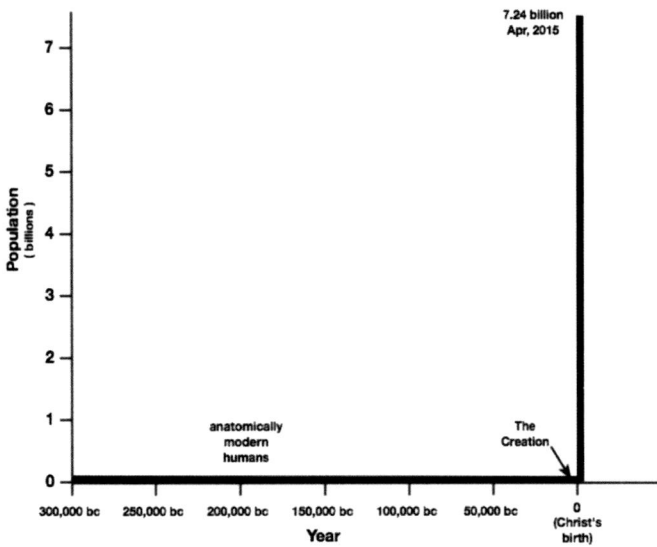

Figure 3.2

Of his Figure 5.1 (our Figure 3.2), Cohen writes:

> The conventional formal portrait of the human popula-
> tion suggests an airport runway that terminates in a high
> stone wall (Figure 5.1). An immensely long period of
> time with very low numbers of people (the runway) is
> followed by a very short period of nearly vertical increase
> in numbers (the wall). Any airplane with a trajectory for
> takeoff like this would severely wrench its passengers and
> its mechanical parts.[90]

Second, in Figure 3.3 the horizontal scale is zoomed in *again*, 10 times
this time, to magnify the rightmost 10 percent of Figure 3.2. For reference,
the approximate time of the cave paintings at Lascaux is shown and the
approximate date of Creation is repeated.

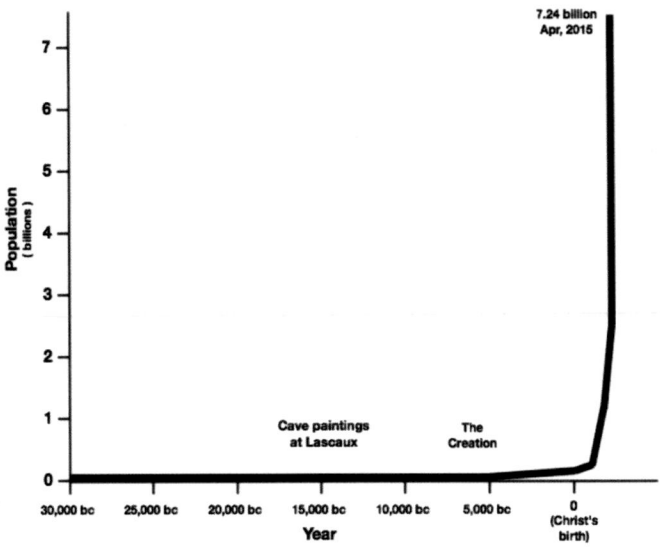

Figure 3.3

Third, in Figure 3.4 the horizontal scale is zoomed in yet again to magnify the rightmost third of Figure 3.3, and show about the rightmost 3 percent of Figure 3.2 (and about the rightmost 1 percent of Cohen's original).

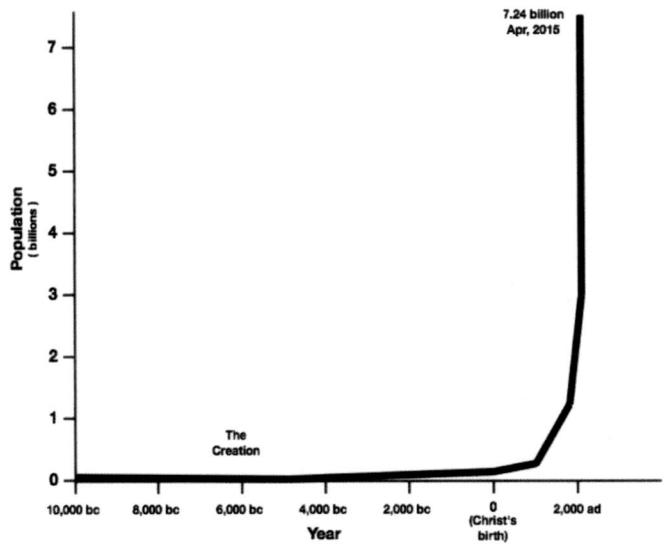

Figure 3.4

Figures 3.2 through 3.4 are visibly crude because they were constructed by hand with data from Cohen's Appendix 2 to illustrate the point that almost 92 percent (6,640 million of 7,240 million) of this population curve has sprung up in the last 300 years, less than the blink of a geologic eye.[91] Put another way, the population has grown by over 1,200 percent (600 million to 7.24 billion) in those 300 years. But this is not news. Carlo Cipolla presented a remarkably similar graph a generation (35 years) ago.[92]

This rapid rise in population cannot be attributed to a single cause or even to a small cluster of causes. On such graphs, however, it is possible to see that the upturn in the population curve lies close to the beginning of the Industrial Era and the Agricultural Revolution.

> The most prolific evidence of the Industrial Revolution's impact on the modern world is seen in the worldwide human population growth. ... The world's human population ... would reach one billion in 1800. ... The birth of the Industrial Revolution altered medicine and living standards, resulting in the population explosion that would commence at that point and steamroll into the 20th and 21st centuries. In only 100 years after the onset of the Industrial Revolution, the world population would grow 100 percent to two billion people in 1927 ... .
>
> During the 20th century, the world population would take on exponential proportions, growing to six billion people just before the start of the 21st century. That's a 400% population increase in a single century.[93] Since the 250 years from the beginning of the Industrial Revolution until today, the world human population has increased by six billion people![94]

WHAT DOES ALL THIS MEAN?

As holders of the Earth's point of view and the top link of the intelligence chain, what are we called to do, if anything? Of primary importance for the physician is the instruction, First, Do No Harm. That guideline incorporates at least four of the 10 Commandments (6–Do Not Kill, 7–Do Not Commit Adultery, 8–Do Not Steal, 9–Do Not Bear False Witness), in just four words. How do we honor this clear but complex matter of care?

Some societies already work under a handicap because they see the self as an individual with rights rather than as a collective with responsibilities. Harold Coward, at the beginning of Chapter 4 of *Visions of a New Earth,* speaks to the ethical implications of seeing the self as individual rather than collective. He writes:

> Most modern Western ethical analysis in matters of reproduction, consumption, and ecology assumes that the ethical agent is 'the choosing individual.' ... I want to critically examine this assumption and suggest that it has two potential flaws: (1) it does not fit with many traditional religious societies where the ethical agent is seen to be the collective rather than the individual; and (2) the focus on the choosing individual as the ethical agent leads to a concentration on rights rather than obligations ... . Both of these points can be interpreted as 'flaws' if they lead to a separation of the individual from the larger context of humanity or nature in which he or she is an interdependent part. ... the modern Western focus on the choosing individual and his or her rights has achieved many positive gains ... these gains—valuable though they are—have had a price, namely, the loss of our sense of collective interrelationships with other humans and with the natural environment that makes our continued life possible.[95,96]

Residents of developed countries may also have difficulty seeing the connection between their individual actions and environmental damage simply because the damage results from the accumulated behavior of a gazillion individuals and is kept well out of sight. Unfortunately, the cumulative impact of our numbers is largely being addressed with technology. But like the feeding of No-Face in *Spirited Away*, technology has only stimulated our appetite for technology:[97]

- we address the need for housing by going denser and higher;
- we address the need for food by adopting agribusiness, chemicals, mono-culture, and gene manipulation;
- we address the hunger for stuff with cheaper offshore labor, debt, big box stores, delivery services, and, finally, self-storage;
- we address the need for more jobs by proposing work time reduction;[98]
- we address the need for education by online courses and mountains of debt;
- we address the need for face-to-face contact with thumb-to-thumb "contact"; and
- we address the need for long-distance travel with larger planes packed overfull.

None of these accommodations address the root common to all of them—a large and growing population. In using technology to address a numbers problem, we have introduced problems with dignity and quality of life. As more people share the planet, each individual wields less influence and Maslow's esteem needs take a beating.

INTERCONNECTION

Sallie McFague speaks eloquently to the matter of our relationship with the Earth in her book *The Body of God*. First, she says sin is the refusal to accept our place; that is, sin is the denial of our interconnection with all Creation. She writes

> The common creation story gives us a functional, working cosmology ... [and] ... has for many people immediate credibility upon first hearing.

Then she offers this meditation:

> So this is where I, we, fit, not as a little lower than the angels but as an inspirited body among other living bodies, one with some distinctive and marvelous characteristics and some genuine limitations. I am of the earth, a product of its ancient and awesome history, and I really and truly belong here. But I am only one among millions,

now billions of other human beings, who have a place, a space on the earth. I am also a member of one species among millions, perhaps billions, of other species that need places on the earth. We are all, human beings and other species, inhabitants of the same space, planet earth, and interdependent in intricate and inexorable ways. I feel a sense of comfort, of settledness, of belonging as I consider my place in this cosmology, but also a sense of responsibility, for I know that I am a citizen of the planet. I have an expanded horizon as I reflect on my place in the common creation story: I belong not only to my immediate family or country or even my species, but to the earth and all its life-forms. I *do* belong to this whole. I know this now. The question is can I, will I, *live* as if I did? Will I accept my proper place in the scheme of things? Will *we*, the human beings of the planet, do so?[99]

ENDNOTE

The New York Times gathered a few short opinions under the title 'is-overpopulation-a-legitimate-threat-to-humanity-and-the-planet'? Here are some of those responses:

> Ehrlich's [Paul Ehrlich, author of *The Population Bomb*] argument that expanding human populations cannot be sustained on an Earth with finite carrying capacity is irrefutable and, indeed, almost tautological. The only uncertainty concerns the timing and severity of the rebalancing that must inevitably occur.[100]

Note that a factor increasing the need for rebalancing is not mentioned here. It is the accumulation of wastes (such as plastics, and nuclear or bio-chemical contaminations) that must either stop being generated, be transformed, or be endured as poisons.

> Regions with very large youth cohorts are historically far more prone to violence than older populations.

Today, population growth is most rapid in precisely such places, mainly in sub-Saharan Africa and the Middle East.[101]

While this is true, it does not mention that the impact of a baby in the developed world is many times more stressful on the Earth than a baby in the developing world.

> The bottom line is that we cannot create a sustainable world unless we empower women to control their own bodies and give them the tools they need to do so. Upholding the human rights of women is essential in balancing both fears of so-called overpopulation and underpopulation.[102]
>
> Because the most important lesson we've learned about population is this: Women's rights are key. Where women have the means and the power to make their own decisions about childbearing, they have smaller (and healthier, and better educated) families.[103]
>
> So saving the world depends not on persuading poor women in distant countries to have fewer babies. They are already doing that. The challenge is to fix capitalism by encouraging innovation in the technologies that can deliver a livable world.[104]

This comment is intriguing, but it feels narrow in two ways. First, technology does not address the root of the problem, it empowers continued behavior and growth. Second, 215,000,000 women have unmet needs for contraception every year.[105]

> A new economic model must account for three major adjustments: First, it must accept limits to growth due to resource constraints and thus ensure resources are priced to reflect their true cost. Second, the economy needs to be subservient to maintaining the vitality of the resource base, and not the other way around, as it is now. Third, an effective economy for the 21st century must weigh collective welfare over individual rights.[106]

These are difficult ideas for those who see the self as an individual with rights rather than as a community member with responsibilities. The recent rise of far-right policies around the world seems to favor those who see themselves as individuals with rights.

An explicit intent of these Pieces is to begin a conversation about population and about protecting and nurturing a diverse, healthy, long-lived planet. Such a conversation will be just the beginning of a fundamental shift in *everything*. Great fear and grief and anger may well accompany this shift. Elisabeth Kubler-Ross has written extensively on the process that accompanies such transitions.[107] Roy Scranton, in his book *Learning to Die in the Anthropocene,* has said clearly that this civilization must come to terms with the fact that it is dying.[108] Rilke and Berry have set out the destination: households, in peace.[109]

More people, all living longer, our planet already under stress for food, water, space, and peace … this begs discussion now. The Fourth Piece considers some of the ways that both Nature and human beings have addressed the issue of population.

FOURTH PIECE

Discussing the Common Factor

It's not enough to just point out the problem.

INTENTION

The First Piece presents that life is a gift, as if of a higher power. It reflects on the goodness of fit of human beings with the Earth and how to respond.

The Second Piece presents that humans are at the top of the intelligence chain and examines the implications of being at the top.

The Third Piece inventories many of the current environmental issues afflicting the Earth. It finds population to be a factor common to each issue.

This Fourth Piece faces the common factor, mentioning some of the ways nature and humans affect both animal and human populations.

THE COMMON FACTOR

From the beginning until the mid-1400s human population fluctuated at less than 500 million. It grew slowly for about the next 350 years and in about 1800 began an unprecedented climb. In the next 200 years it increased more than sevenfold and is projected to pass ninefold in about one more generation. (See Figure 2.4)

The reason that the population curve was so flat for hundreds of thousands of years (up until the mid-1400s) has much to do with the high death rate. Predation, starvation, illness, exposure, and hard choice (infanticide to benefit the group) all combined to restrain population growth. Most of these factors are still present (except for predation and perhaps exposure), but they no longer restrain population as they once did.

This Fourth Piece can only note, barely and in passing, some of the factors that influence populations. After the 1700s, it took only two to three centuries for human population to get to its current size. The reasons are complex and intertwined, but growth was largely unfettered thanks to the revolution in food production. The path forward will also be complex and—whether population increases or declines, whether we walk in global cooperation or not—will be full of contention and suffering.

CLARIFYING TERMS

It's difficult to find the right word(s) to label this topic – Population *what? Control* has bad vibes all around it, as do *Regulation, Constraint*, and even *Restraint. Management* feels like a politically correct version of *Control.* Population *Connection* is already taken and carries only a loose association (verbally) with a large and growing number of people. *Awareness, Sensitivity*, and *Balance* do not seem to say enough. Population *Reduction* is direct and to the point, but stirs defensive and existential tremors, as do *Suppression, Abatement, Curtailment*, and *De-population.*

The above is overdone, but the question is real. What do we call this sensitive, necessarily emotional opinion that claims that there are too many people? Too many for all of us to have an acceptable quality of life, of liberty, of pursuit of happiness. Let alone space to stretch out, nap, and picnic with enough to eat.

The Earth and its life are suffering; much of this suffering is in direct proportion to the number of people and our domination of the biosphere. So, from here these Pieces will refer to this issue of population size as Population *Care. Care* with its meanings of having regard for, making provision for, looking out for, taking care of. *Care* with its meanings of concern and compassion. *Care* with its understanding that unexamined population growth is not healthy for either humans or the Earth.

POPULATION CARE

This is a difficult Piece, because it deals directly with death. It's hard reading, given the wide variety of ways to die, the suffering of whole groups of life, and our ability to tolerate or turn away from that suffering when it happens to others.

If you look at Figure 2.4, you see that nature cared for (managed) population well until about the mid-18th century. "Managed well" in this case means that a high death rate kept human population in balance with the birth rate, with resources, and with other life. Predation, starvation, illness, natural disaster, concern for group survival, and even evolution held down population growth.[110]

None of these factors by themselves have a large effect on population growth now. Even cumulatively they have only a modest effect. But they are important to see listed because eventually humans' combination of mental and physical abilities along with their fertility bent their population curve upward, growing open-ended and vertically ever since.

This Piece speaks first to the care of populations by nature and then by humans themselves. Nature's care usually plays out over generations spread over centuries. It involves no planning and is amoral, largely unpredictable, episodic, and (except for disasters) glacial. What follows is not complete in either the big or small pictures, it simply hints at the complexity of population care.

NATURE'S CARE OF BOTH ANIMAL AND HUMAN POPULATIONS

Nature is a well-known though fuzzily defined concept, but its impact is real and it affects both humans and all other creatures together; indeed, nature brought us here. This Piece includes discussion of both animal and human populations because

- humans are animals,
- all animals are co-dependent and share the Earth,
- nature's care directly affects all animals, and

• the more humans the more of certain animals (as food, companions, service aids, and pests), and the fewer of certain other animals (particularly those whose habitats are lost and those who are eliminated as undesirable or dismissed as unnecessary).

PREDATION

Of the five major hazards mentioned here, predation no longer threatens humans as it did on the savanna, even though genocides still occur with the purpose of destroying a population group or culture.

On the savanna, humans were prey. That we are still here is due in part because those predators had planning only as complex as stalking-when-hungry. Gradually, as humans changed from migratory to settled, those predators have had less and less impact on human survival. With the advent of various weapons and the capacity for planning, humans themselves have become the top predator.

At the tiny end of the size spectrum, various bacteria, viruses, and parasites can, from the human point of view, be called predators. Though they can multiply and mutate, they can't be said to plan. Through healthcare, antibiotics, and antiviral drugs their role in population care seesaws up and down.

In the middle of the size spectrum, spiders build webs and snakes slither, but webs seem evidence less of planning than of stationary stalking and slithering merely scent-guided stalking-when-hungry.

Chimpanzees, crows, orangutans, elephants, and others use tools, but humans' ability to plan lets them prey on the whole spectrum: animals and other humans alike.[111]

STARVATION

Starvation affects humans and animals in separate ways but indiscriminately. Johan Rockstrom and Martin Klum, in their book *Big World Small Planet* note that about 11,700 years ago:

Humanity literally came in from the cold into a remarkably stable warm environment. ...

Almost as soon as we entered the Holocene, groups of hunters and gatherers in at least four different parts of the world independently invented agriculture more or less simultaneously. ...

The onset of the Holocene, in short, was the planetary equivalent of establishing the ultimate shopping mall for humanity.[112]

With the first pivots described by Ruth DeFries in *The Big Ratchet,* the ability to provide food fueled human population rise. Humans are described by DeFries as a species in a perpetual scramble for food. She lays out a cycle of ratchet-hatchet-pivots to describe the continuing advance of our species, particularly with regard to food production. A ratchet is the increase in food production to solve the current needs of the population. A hatchet is the crisis that develops as the benefits of this ratchet are used up by a growing population. A pivot represents the introduction of the next paradigm shift in food production.[113]

The Big Ratchet presents the ratchet and pivot as a measure of hope for humanity, but does not much mention the suffering of the hatchet. DeFries speaks of humanity as a whole when she notes the long struggle to survive. But generalizing about humanity's struggle glosses over an enormous amount of suffering during the hatchet, when entire cultures and civilizations have died off.[114] It's worth noting that humans, as well as nature, can purposely bring about the suffering of a hatchet—an estimated 20 million people died of starvation during China's Great Leap Forward.[115]

Modern agriculture has broken through the recent constraints to food production through the use of carbon-based energy to till, plant, fertilize, harvest, process, and distribute food. Carbon based energy also creates and distributes the chemicals and GMOs that approximate the resources that nature used to provide, but which result in significant waste and pollution along with their productivity gains.

Some would say we are in a ratchet period now, with more calories available per person than ever.[116] Others would say we are in a hatchet, with a billion people going to bed hungry each night and 7.6 million (1.25

million of them children) starving to death each year.[117] On the one hand, it's not known how long the Earth can support this rate of food production and chronic suffering. On the other hand, food waste is epidemic, obesity is rampant, distribution is spotty, and the quality of those available calories can be questionable.

Hunger was a major limit to population when it was understood and respected on the savanna. Our pre-agriculture ancestors understood the power of hunger to the point of using infanticide to balance the group's numbers with the available food supply. Currently we have come to expect continued pivots to solve food problems and to expect better distribution to solve hunger problems. But the situation is complex, for even when distribution is ideal poverty may prevent millions from getting food.

INFECTIOUS DISEASE

Illness is the referee between bacteria and antibiotics: surviving an illness awards victory to antibiotics and dying awards victory to bacteria. Antibiotics have become such a factor in food farming that treatment of food animals with prophylactic antibiotics is routine. Even so, the factory approach to providing food has its hazards and vulnerabilities. The gathering of large numbers of animals together leaves them vulnerable to epidemics of communicable diseases, especially those that resist the antibiotics or have no vaccine. *The New York Times* reported in May 2015 that some 33 million birds were in flocks exposed to bird flu and were to be euthanized to control the virus' spread.[118] Bill Gates has stated concern for an epidemic within the next decade, given the rise of antimicrobial resistance to drugs and weaknesses in the global emergency response system.[119]

A couple of decades ago when Joel Cohen wrote *How Many People Can the Earth Support*, he included a section *Time constraints in infectious disease: Will AIDS solve the population problem?* Not that many *months* ago that section could have read ... *Will EBOLA solve the population problem?*

As the Earth becomes more crowded and more people move into already densely packed cities, communicable diseases become a major threat. Airline flights take that threat global. As this is written, the concern is the Zika virus and its possible link to serious brain defects. Two centuries ago Zika would have been another small step in evolution—one full of individual suffering, but from an evolutionary point of view just another agent of natural selection.

NATURAL DISASTER

The website *www.ready.gov/natural-disasters* lists the following (alphabetically) as natural disasters: drought, earthquake, extreme heat, flood, home fire, hurricane, landslide and debris flow, severe weather, space weather, thunderstorms and lightning, tornadoes, tsunamis, volcanoes, wildfires, winter storms and extreme cold. Wikipedia lists six categories of natural disasters with a combined total of 16 types.[120]

A growing population guarantees that people both with and without wealth or insurance will move into areas at high risk for natural disasters. Forests and deserts, canyon cliffs, the top and bottom of mudslide-prone hills, the beach front and riverside properties, the reclaimed landfills, the tornado alleys, the volcanic flow paths, the denied, ignored, and unknown fault lines—all will fill up with people desperate for place.

When extreme weather strikes, causing displacement and loss, women, girls, and the LGBTQ have an increased risk of exposure to physical and sexual violence. After a tsunami in the Solomon Islands displaced 10,000 people, women and girls in temporary campsites reported an increase in violence and that they felt unsafe bathing or traveling to get water. In some cases, women may avoid using emergency shelters altogether because of the threat of violence and harassment.[121]

Extreme weather is becoming more common. It will be expensive too.

> ... in Miami Beach. ... the city has elevated eight roads, raised six sea walls and installed 10 massive pumps to push flood waters back into Biscayne Bay. That $100 million investment is the first installment on a $400 million gamble that will, over the next few years, elevate another two miles of street and install 70 more pumps. ... But these engineering fixes are likely just a prelude to bolder innovations: Planners have already proposed radical-sounding ideas like floating personal islands and

even waterproofing whole portions of the peninsula. If the gamble pays off, it won't solve the problems that sea-level rise poses for Miami Beach. It will only buy the city some time. ...

There are 417 condo towers—a total of 50,060 units—currently under construction from Miami to West Palm Beach. And not one of those towers has been built to plans that take sea level rise into account, say land-use attorneys, politicians and other authorities.[122]

NATURAL SELECTION (EVOLUTION)

A story of nature's population care through evolution is told in the matter of Isle Royale, an isolated island off the coast of Lake Superior. It hosts a relatively straightforward single predator single-prey relationship between wolf and moose which has been studied in detail for over 50 years. Here humans took care not to interfere with nature. This relationship is the subject of a textbook lab exercise showing the theoretical behavior when a predator arrives to help balance a blooming (in this case, moose) population.[123]

The Wikipedia entry for the current situation on Isle Royale tells a story that is more real, more complex, and sadder than that of the lab exercise. Rather than settling down to the cyclical balancing portrayed in the lab exercise, the real-world populations of both wolf and moose have fluctuated wildly. The current wolf population has dwindled due to inbreeding, which has negatively affected their ability to hunt. The moose population has grown, overeaten its healthiest food, and is seesawing up and down, dependent on an inferior food source. The moose population will now most likely be controlled by starvation during the winter. The wolf population will most likely die out.[124]

Research by Michael Nelson of Oregon State University reports on public comments solicited by the National Park Service. They reveal that 86 percent of those surveyed agree that wolves should be present on Isle Royale—even if that means intervening on their behalf. Nelson says, "We're trying to understand the moral reasoning behind those preferences."[125]

HUMANS' CARE OF ANIMAL POPULATIONS

Animal populations are managed by humans to provide food, to ensure fish, fowl, and game for sport, to provide animals for experimentation, to provide companions and service animals, and to control populations of feral animals and those considered pests. These practices bring us face to face with our responsibility at the top of the intelligence chain, for we gauge life's value by how other species' intelligence compares with ours. For instance, consider the difference in outcry that would result from eating insects versus fish versus chickens versus cows versus dogs or cats versus an ape who can sign.

ANIMALS AS FOOD

As little as a hundred years ago it was common to prepare one's own food from animals that one had bred and raised oneself, or to personally destroy animals suffering from disease or accidents or predators' attacks. It was a culturally familiar practice that most participated in because they lived on farms where this was a necessary part of life.

Now raising animals for food goes on outside of most people's awareness, our closest contact being the curved Plexiglas meat counter in the grocery store. Fast food restaurants support massive beef, pork, chicken, and fish production which can only be described as food factories. These factories came into being to support a growing population hungry for fast, cheap food. Will this approach be retired when science and technology develop a way to process vats of chemicals (perhaps with the help of genetically modified bacteria) to make protein that's indistinguishable from animal protein?[126]

ANIMALS AS GAME FOR SPORT

Nations, states, and counties all routinely license hunting and fishing to control the availability and abundance of game animals. The regulations governing these licenses are complex, having to account for estimates of wild populations, weather, the animals' food supply, habitat loss, hunters' demand, natural disaster, the rights of local and native peoples, and potentially conflicting regulations. California, and many other areas in the world, publishes regulations for freshwater sport fishing, ocean sport fishing, commercial fishing, mammal hunting, and bird hunting that limit the times and amounts of killing permitted.[127] Hunters understand, support, and abide by these restrictions, but such regulations are under-enforced worldwide, as implied in the killing of Cecil the lion and the many documentaries on poaching. Our tendency (as evidenced by the destruction of passenger pigeons, buffalo, beaver, baby seals, elephants, rhinos, etc.) is to dominate other creatures with little concern other than economic.

ANIMALS AS SUBJECTS FOR EXPERIMENTS

Animals are used in scientific and medical research labs, which raise populations of animals under carefully controlled conditions for drug and chemical testing. These animals are well cared for to ensure their health and uniformity so that experiments are dependable and repeatable. Lines of lab animals have been modified to enable research on animals closer to humans than they otherwise would be. Genetic modification is happening both through gene splicing and crossbreeding to change the characteristics of plants and animals for human purposes.[128]

At the same time, computer programs and knowledge bases are closing in on realistic simulations and models of human organs, life processes, and diseases. And technology is making progress at laboratory growth of organs for testing and eventual transplantation without harming a live creature.

ANIMALS FOR SERVICE OR COMPANIONSHIP

The Americans with Disabilities Act (ADA) defines service animals as dogs only.

> *Service animals are defined as dogs that are individually trained to do work or perform tasks for people with disabilities.* Examples of such work or tasks include guiding people who are blind, alerting people who are deaf, pulling a wheelchair, alerting and protecting a person

who is having a seizure, reminding a person with mental illness to take prescribed medications, calming a person with Post Traumatic Stress Disorder (PTSD) during an anxiety attack, or performing other duties. Service animals are working animals, not pets. The work or task a dog has been trained to provide must be directly related to the person's disability. Dogs whose sole function is to provide comfort or emotional support do not qualify as service animals under the ADA.

This definition does not affect or limit the broader definition of "assistance animal" under the Fair Housing Act or the broader definition of "service animal" under the Air Carrier Access Act.

Some State and local laws also define service animal more broadly than the ADA does. Information about such laws can be obtained from that State's attorney general's office.[129]

A *pet* or *companion animal* is an animal kept primarily for a person's company or protection, as opposed to working animals, sport animals, livestock, and laboratory animals, which are kept primarily for performance, agricultural value, or research. ...

There is a medically approved class of therapy animals, mostly dogs or cats, that are brought to visit confined humans. Pet therapy utilizes trained animals and handlers to achieve specific physical, social, cognitive, and emotional goals with patients.[130]

Though the number of these animals directly tracks the human population, it's hard to think of them as causing crowding or suffering because of their numbers.

ANIMAL OVERPOPULATION

Animal population management is used in a manner often considered negative to deal with the overabundance of domestic pets and companion animals that end up in Humane Society clinics and shelters or loose on the street. Some large dog and cat neutering clinics offer their services free or for low cost in an attempt to minimize the need for terminations. Veterinarians often accomplish the humane termination of animals that are suffering, whether from illness or accident or debilitating old age.

It's also possible to cause suffering through non-management of a natural condition, though in one particular case much, if not most, of the suffering happens to humans. The story of peacocks in Palos Verdes, California is a complex interaction of large, sometimes quite aggressive birds, the people who like them and the people who don't, plus ample food (human supplied) and a lack of natural predators. The birds' shrieks cause sleepless nights, and they are big and strong enough to damage roofs of both cars and houses. Enough birds have been found dead of suspicious causes that there is now a $200,000 fine for killing one.[131,132] The story is only funny from a safe distance.

ANIMALS AS PESTS

Population management of animals by humans is used in a negative manner (or positive, depending on your point of view) to control those creatures thought of as pests. Other animals and pets sickened and killed after encountering poisoned pests are considered unfortunate collateral damage. Sometimes this collateral damage affects an innocent but essential animal, as with the suspected link between the use of neonicotinoids and the collapse of bee colonies and populations.

The domination we exert over creatures labeled as pests causes their suffering in direct proportion to our numbers and our distaste (or our taste). Articles are appearing about the raising of insects for food.[133] The name for insect eating is *entomophagy*. It is not the purpose here to argue either for or against any of these practices, but to note that they are an ongoing part of life that is seldom publicly acknowledged or examined. Yet even a casual examination reveals how closely tied they are with our choices about life and death, nuisance, and health.

HUMANS' CARE OF HUMAN POPULATIONS

There are more ways that humans care and have cared for themselves than first come to mind. It's a hard topic to face, for it's threatening and we try not to think about it. Some care is imposed externally by government or social pressure; some arises internally within the individual. The methods discussed here include religion, policy, persuasion, self-reflection, personal choice, infanticide, genocide, suicide, fantasy, science fiction, movies, and contraception.

SOME GIVENS
GENESIS

We live in a collection of givens that are nearly as invisible to us as water is to fish. A primary given rises from invitations such as those of Genesis 1:28, 8:17, 9:1-3, and 9:7. In Genesis 1:28, man and woman are blessed and told to multiply and to subdue and rule over the Earth. In Genesis 8:17, Noah gathers all creatures to the ark so that they, too, may ultimately breed abundantly. And in Genesis 9:1-3, after the cleansing flood has subsided, this injunction is repeated to Noah and his sons this way:

> And God blessed Noah and his sons and said to them,
> "Be fruitful and multiply, and fill the earth.
> The fear of you and the terror of you will be on every beast
> of the earth and on every bird of the sky; with everything
> that creeps on the ground, and all the fish of the sea, into
> your hand they are given.
> Every moving thing that is alive shall be food for you; I
> give it all to you, as I gave the green plant. …"

It is a dark blessing to learn that you will terrorize every beast of the Earth and every bird of the sky, and that you may eat every moving, living thing.

In Genesis 9:7 God repeats a third time his encouragement for life:

> As for you, be fruitful and multiply; populate the earth
> abundantly and multiply in it.

One effect of such givens can be seen in the Palestinian–Israeli race to out-proliferate each other, as told in the first few pages of *Countdown*.[134] And it's seen in the determination of radical sects to subjugate the world by force and rape, current in the news. And it's seen in Figure 2.4.

The questions such givens raise are clear:

- Who decides when the Earth is full?
- Who tells everyone?
- Who carries out this conclusion?

These questions beg global discussion because to voice the idea that the planet is full, that it's time to end unfettered reproduction is to jolt awake unspeakable indignation and righteousness. And yet the decision to not have another child is happening—one family, one couple at a time around the world, especially where contraceptives are freely available or where sexual restraint is necessary. After all, the biblical injunctions to fill the Earth were written at a time when the world was flat and the center of everything; when *galaxy* was not yet a glimmer of a word; when high speed was tens of miles per day, communication was by word of mouth, news of distant countries was at most of academic interest, the known population was perhaps 300 million, and entire continents with their native peoples were unknown.

AWARENESS OF SELF

Another given is the tendency of developed nations to see self as individual rather than as community. This can lead to a significant focus on rights and entitlements and a devaluation of obligations and responsibilities.[135] Having rights and entitlement empowers certainty and "Certainty breeds tremendous smugness."[136]

When the self is seen as the community, our interconnections with each other are honored and obligations and responsibilities are respected. The small sacrifices required for the benefit of the community are just that—small. Garrison Keillor noted that life in a small town had a strong socialist aspect—rather than drive miles to the mall, you patronized the local store because you knew its owner, and each employee, and their families' circumstances.

RELIGION

In a papal bull issued May 4, 1493, Pope Alexander VI granted the King and Queen of Castille a decree that all newly discovered lands west of an imaginary line of longitude running through the eastern part of present-day Brazil belonged to Spain, and everything east to Portugal.[137] Over the years this Papal Bull has become the basis by which the Native American populations were decimated.[138,139] The book *Pagans in the Promised Land* by Steven Newcomb uses cognitive theory to decode, disassemble, and challenge this doctrine of Christian discovery and domination.[140]

Recently, Ruth DeFries has written:

> The English interpreted the decimation wrought by Old World diseases as divine providence. King James 1620 charter granted "the planting, ruling, ordering, and governing of New England in America" to the Plymouth Company, claiming that "God's visitation reigned a wonderful plague ... so that there is not left ... any that doe claime or challenge any Kind of Interests therein."[141]

What a tragic interpretation of communicable disease.

The story of Iran over a period of less than 35 years illustrates the influence religious leaders can have over fertility. In Iran in 1979 there were 37 million Iranians and a functioning family planning program. War with Iraq (1980–1988) brought an end to family planning and initiated a religiously sponsored campaign to birth an army. This campaign went so well that Weisman writes:

> As the war with Iraq dragged on, the birth rate surpassed Khomeini's demographic dreams. ... By some estimates, the growth rate peaked at 4.2 %, near the biological limits for fertile women. ...
>
> Khomeini's divine mandate spawned as breathtaking a demographic leap as the world had ever seen—which made what came next all the more astonishing. ...[142]

The war had exhausted and nearly bankrupted the country; to feed, educate, house, and employ this new population would far outstrip their capacity. So shortly after the war ended, the mullahs and the media took up a new slogan—One is good, two is enough. Imam Khomeini died in 1989. Only 12 years later the Iranian Minister of Health accepted the UN Population Award for the most enlightened and successful approach to family planning the world had ever seen.

> Everyone wanted to know how such a thing could happen in a Muslim nation—and with a voluntary program, no less.
>
> There was no covert coercion, she'd [Dr. Hourieh Shamshiri, a deputy in Iran's Ministry of Health] explain. The sole requirement was that all couples attend premarital classes held in mosques or in health centers where couples went for prenuptial blood tests. The classes taught contraception and sex education, and stressed the advantages of having fewer children to feed, clothe, and school. The only governmental disincentive was elimination of the individual subsidy for food, electricity, telephone, and appliances for any child after the first three.
>
> By 2000, Iran's total fertility rate reached replacement level, ... a year faster than China's compulsory one-child policy. In 2012, it was 1.7.[143]

What had happened was simply the most stunning reversal of purposeful population growth in human history, all in response to religious leaders' influence.

POLICY

Worldwatch Institute presents nine policy points important to voluntary population care[144]:

- Provide universal access to safe and effective contraceptive options for both sexes.
- Guarantee education through secondary school for all, especially girls.
- Eradicate gender bias from law, economic opportunity, health, and culture.
- Offer age-appropriate sexuality education for all students.

- End all policies that reward parents financially based on the number of children they have.
- Integrate lessons on population, environment, and development into school curricula at multiple levels.
- Put prices on environmental costs and impacts.
- Adjust to an aging population instead of boosting childbearing through government incentives and programs.
- Convince leaders to commit to stabilizing population growth through the exercise of human rights and human development.

These nine points are clear, voluntary, and can be effective for both groups and individuals. Bryce Covert, a contributing op-ed writer to the New York Times, has written of the direct link between low or no-cost contraceptives to the economic growth of a nation.[145]

An often-cited example of human population care through policy is China's one-child policy. Mei Fong's book *One Child, The Story of China's Most Radical Experiment,* explores this experiment in detail. A method that can only technically be called persuasion, it was recently rescinded as its ramifications became clear through experience as well as prediction.[146,147]

Fong's book ends with an account of her own attempts to become a mother. She achieved twin boys through in-vitro fertilization, and ends the Epilogue with this:

> One day, I will tell them about a country once so poor, an emperor ruled that each family could have only one child. Of how a great sadness came over the land, and how people gave away their children, or stole other people's, or sought the help of magicians to make their single precious child the strongest and brightest they could. And how it came to pass that there were fewer and fewer babies born to the land, and it became a country of the old.
>
> I don't know the ending to this story.
>
> And then I lie awake as they sleep, the steady rhythm of their breathing the most peaceful and frightening sound in the world.[148]

PERSUASION

In Mexico, telenovelas were used to try to convince the population that smaller families had real benefits. It worked. Figure 4.1 shows Mexico's average annual growth rate over nearly a century.[149]

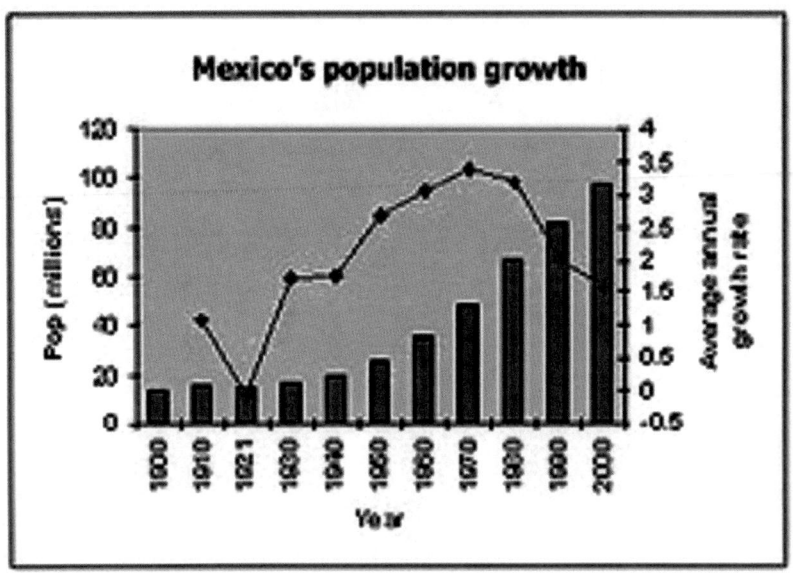

Figure 4.1

Mexico was a pioneer in the 1970s and 1980s using telenovelas to shape behavior, and was particularly successful in introducing the idea of family planning through this method.[150] A similar success for this kind of persuasion came about in Brazil.[151]

SELF-REFLECTION

It's tempting from our present vantage point to say that the time on the savanna must have been soaked in grief, because what kept the population curve flat was a high death rate due to predators, hunger, disease, accidents, and exposure; partnering with those more natural causes was infanticide.

Laura Kipnis argues against this view of being soaked in grief in Chapter 2 of Meghan Daum's book *Selfish, Shallow, and Self-Absorbed: Sixteen Writers on the Decision Not to Have Kids*. Kipnis writes

> It was only as families began getting smaller ... that the emotional value of each child increased. ... All I'm saying is that what we're calling biological instinct [maternal fulfillment] is a historical artifact—a culturally specific development, not a fact of nature.[152]

Kipnis goes on to agree with historian Philippe Ariès in saying that childhood is less a recognizable concept than a social invention.

Penny Spikins, however, argues that there is archeological evidence for compassion in early humans:

> ... in this volume Penny Spikins argues that compassion lies at the heart of what makes us human. She takes us on a journey from the earliest stone age societies two million years ago to the lives of Neanderthals in Ice Age Europe, using archaeological evidence to illustrate the central role that emotional connections had in human evolution. Simple acts of kindness left to us from millions of years ago provide evidence for how social emotions and morality evolved, ...[153]

And a recent *New York Times* article reports on changes that occur in a mother's brain during pregnancy. They are a possible reason for mothers' increased ability to perceive the perspectives and feelings of others.[154]

Sometimes self-reflection occurs at the group level, especially where self is seen as community. Alan Rabinowitz followed a story about a small group of about 150 families of Asian pigmies, the Taron, living in a nearly inaccessible Himalayan valley.[155] He found a single survivor of the group, Dawi, who said that as the group shrank they suffered various birth defects that arose through inbreeding. The elders held council and charged Dawi, the last intact male, to allow the line to die out.[156] A Wikipedia article included in this reference mentions that Dawi initially agreed, but later announced he would travel to Tibet or Yunnan, China in order to search for a wife, since many Taron/Dulong people lived there. Dawi's elders most likely knew of their relatives in Tibet and China, nevertheless it must have been a heartbreaking decision to declare the local population at an end.

© Steve Winter/National Geographic

Figure 4.2

Alan with Dawi

PERSONAL CHOICE

In a brief interview with a professional Korean woman, she told the author that neither she nor any of her siblings had had or currently wanted any children. She said that in her case she had wanted a child when she was younger and married, but her husband didn't. Now she's single and feels she's past the age for having a healthy child. So she, along with her siblings, are living life while looking out for each other. She later added that the majority of her friends were also childless.

On the back cover of Meghan Daum's book *Selfish, Shallow and Self-Absorbed*, Hannah Pittard, author of *Reunion* and *The Fates Will Find Their Way* writes this:

> I've never needed approval for my decision to go child-
> less through this world, but there've been times when
> I wanted company, a sounding board, a friend who
> wouldn't take the wrong way my desire to be occasionally

ecstatic about not having babies and all the opportunities it affords me.[157]

Pat Buchanan sees this no-children choice in a different light. In his book *The Death of the West* he writes:

> The West is dying. Its nations have ceased to reproduce, and their populations have stopped growing and begun to shrink. ... Today, in seventeen European countries there are more burials than births, more coffins than cradles. The countries are Belgium, Bulgaria, Croatia, the Czech Republic, Denmark, Estonia, Germany, Hungary, Italy, Latvia, Lithuania, Portugal, Romania, Slovakia, Slovenia, Spain, and Russia.[158]

Note that it's a misreading of the data to say that these countries have ceased to reproduce or to say that their populations have begun to shrink. Figure 4.1 shows a drop in growth rate while the population still increases as those women born in previous years come of childbearing age (ages 15 to 44). Nor does Buchanan mention the Western countries with Total Fertility Rates (TFRs) above replacement level.[159]

A recent study found the percent of unplanned children still hung at about 35 percent in the United States. According to one study, over one third of living people in the United States under 31 years of age (born since 1982) were the result of unintended pregnancies, a rate that has remained largely unchanged to date.[160]

Some have trumpeted congratulations at our reduced teen and unplanned pregnancy rates:[161]

> Teen births are at the lowest ever reported in the USA and both the number of births and birth rate dropped 10% in just one year, according to fresh federal data released today.
>
> The number of births to teens ages 15-19 in 2013 was 274,641, which the National Center for Health Statistics says is the lowest since it started tracking such data from all states in 1933. That number is far fewer than in 1970, which was the all-time peak year with 644,708 teen births.

> The 10% drop in the teen birth rate – to 26.6 births
> per 1,000 from 29.4 births per 1,000 in 2012 -- marked
> another historic low. ...

This decrease in the United States teenage birth rate is a fine success, but when you compare it to Western Europe, you see that there's more to be done:

Despite the drastic drops in U.S. teen birth rates, Haub [Carl Haub, senior demographer of the nonprofit Population Reference Bureau] notes that the new low of 26.6 is 5.5 times higher than in Western Europe, where rates are in single digits. The most recent United Nations data shows Switzerland at a low of 1.9 and Luxembourg at a high of 8.3, with most others in the area at 5 or 6 per 1,000 teens.

An unplanned pregnancy is one that the woman herself said she was not intending. The problem of unplanned pregnancy is not limited to teenagers. We have this from The National Campaign, an organization committed to prevention of teen and unplanned pregnancies:

> Although teen pregnancy is a well-recognized problem,
> the larger challenge of unplanned, unintended preg-
> nancy among non-teens is poorly understood. Among
> teens the primary question is what to do? Among non-
> teens, the question is, what is the problem and why
> should I care? At present, fully *half of all pregnancies* are
> described by women themselves as unplanned. Among
> unmarried women in their twenties, 7 in 10 pregnancies
> are unplanned. As is true for teen pregnancy, unplanned
> pregnancy—especially among single young adults—car-
> ries with it a broad array of socio-economic and health
> risks to women and men, to the children, and to the
> larger community.[162]

Among those unplanned children are the unwanted. The term *unwanted* covers a wide spectrum of rejection, but about the only thing more tragic than an unwanted child is an unwanted orphan.

Wendell Berry writes of the loss of simple restraint with regard to pregnancy:

The sort of restraint I am talking about is illustrated in a recent *National Geographic* article about the people of Hunza in northern Pakistan. The author is a woman, Sabrina Michaud, and she is talking with a Hunza woman in her kitchen:

'What have you done to have only one child?' she asks me. ... 'We leave our husband's bed until each child is weaned, ... but this natural means of birth control has declined, and population has soared.'

Berry goes on to note that

... placed geographically as they were, they lived always in sight of their agricultural or ecological limits, and they made a competent response [until roads and progress broke those limits].[163]

INFANTICIDE

Though considered brutally unacceptable today, infanticide still occurs. It is not unique to humans, but is reported in species ranging from microscopic rotifers through fish and voles and birds to baboons.[164] An article by Anthropologist Laila Williamson indicates that infanticide was a widespread practice both geographically and across time.[165] She notes that

Infanticide has been practiced on every continent and by people on every level of cultural complexity, from hunter gatherers to high civilizations, including our own ancestors. Rather than being an exception, then, it has been the rule.[166]

Reasons for infanticide often center around economic necessity, sometimes for the good of the family and sometimes for the good of the group. Some sense of this group ethic can be found in pre-retreat information passed to the participants in a Bearing Witness retreat on an Indian reservation in South Dakota in the summer of 2015:

Cooperation is highly valued [in Native American communities]. The value placed on cooperation is strongly rooted in the past, when cooperation was necessary for the survival of family and group.[167]

In South Africa the Children's Act does not protect the lives of children and there is no Infanticide Act. Infanticide is rife due to overpopulation, poverty, teenage pregnancy, and rape. Between Johannesburg and Soweto (South Africa's largest township) 200 babies a month are left for dead. Only 60 of those are found alive and taken to a place of safety.[168]

Lest we think South Africa singularly backward, consider Christina Johansdotter. From Wikipedia we read that she was

> ... a Swedish murderer who, in 1740, killed a child in Stockholm with the sole purpose of suicide by execution.
>
> ...
>
> Technically, this avoided the damnation that was promised by most Christian doctrine as a penalty of suicide. Cases such as this were common; to murder a child was a common method used by many suicidal people. ...
>
> In 18th century Sweden, the wish to commit suicide was the most common reason for murdering a child, second only to unmarried women suffocating their newly-born infants after their secret birth.[169]

Or consider baby farming. Baby farmers were women who looked after children for a fee. The term was first used by the *British Medical Journal* in 1867, in an article in which they described a mother who had turned her children over to the baby farmer with the clear understanding that they would be neglected until they died. The majority of baby farmers were caring and honest. A number of them, though, abandoned, starved, or even killed the infants in their care to increase their profits. Until 1872, there were no laws to govern baby farmers. The battle against baby farming was fought more or less continuously from 1865 to 1943. It took 78 years to push through effective legislation to protect the lives of children.[170]

These practices cannot be easily dismissed by saying these are ancestors who lived a long time ago; or because we imagine them as dirty, uneducable savages, without language, intelligence, or feelings; or even because it's so painful to bear witness to such behavior. Infanticide may have been a survival tool pre-agriculture, baby farming may have seemed a social necessity in Victorian times, but to hold the good of the group above the life of one's child or to choose whispered shame as preferable to claiming one's child reflects desperate emotions.

CHILD EUTHANASIA

Euthanasia applied to children who are gravely ill or who suffer from significant birth defects is legal, though controversial, in the Netherlands under rigidly controlled conditions. Some critics have compared child euthanasia to infanticide.[171]

GENOCIDE

The general cannot be fully mourned except through the specific. To just recite the more familiar examples of genocide—Armenian, Holocaust, Bangladesh, Rwandan, Bosnian—is to gloss over and slight their tragedy. And it's to omit our own country's four-century genocide of Native Americans. Native Americans were systematically overrun or discarded and killed from 1492 to 1890. On September 8, 2000, the head of the United States Bureau of Indian Affairs (BIA) formally apologized for the agency's participation in the ethnic cleansing of Western tribes.[172,173,174] In 2016, Wesley Clark, Jr. and Michael Wood, Jr. organized veterans to assist the water protectors at Standing Rock. Clark subsequently made a formal apology to tribal elders for the Army's participation in the genocide.[175,176]

Although Wikipedia lists 27 definitions of genocide, almost all international bodies prosecute genocide based on the Convention on the Prevention and Punishment of the Crime of Genocide (CPPCG), adopted by the UN General Assembly in late 1948.[177]

Wikipedia has an entry for each of these genocides:

- Native American genocide: 1492 to 1890, death of perhaps 54 million,[178]
- Armenian genocide: 1915 to 1917, death of about 1.5 million,[179]
- Holocaust: early to mid 1940s, death of 6 to 11 million,[180]
- Bangladesh genocide: 1971, death of up to 3 million,[181]
- Cambodian genocide: 1975 to 1979, death of around 2 million,[182]

- Kurdish genocide: 1986 to 1989, death of? This link leads to a disambiguation page offering 5 separate choices for clarifying which event is of interest.[183]
- Rwandan genocide: 1994, death of an estimated 0.5 to 1 million,[184]
- Bosnian genocide: 1995, death of about 8,400.[185]

SUICIDE

Some may dismiss suicide as an unimportant factor in population care, for it's unlikely that many individuals kill themselves out of a sense that the Earth is too full. And yet the psychological pressure of a crowded, tumultuous city combined with loss or depression could lead to suicidal thoughts, particularly in the diseased, elderly, handicapped, or helpless.

Currently suicide bombers are terrorizing entire countries. Although many can die in a suicide bombing, it is intended to inspire terror more than manage population.

Some suicides are considered admirable. The story of the 300 Spartan warriors at the battle of Thermopylae is generally regarded as a courageous act and the Alamo is honored as a brave and righteous defiance. Posthumous awards are presented to soldiers such as Army Captain Humayun Khan who sacrificed himself to save his troops.[186]

In a less violent example, euthanasia is being considered under carefully prescribed conditions. A PBS story on January 17, 2015 mentioned Belgium as leading the way in euthanasia, with some 1,800 deaths a year. Since 2009, voluntary euthanasia has been legal in Belgium, Luxembourg, the Netherlands, Switzerland, and the states of Oregon (USA) and Washington (USA).

FANTASY, SCIENCE FICTION, AND MOVIES

Science Fiction is, of course, just that—fiction. And yet it can depict deeply thoughtful scenarios about the future. The book *Love in the Anthropocene* by Jamieson and Nadzam is an example. Five short stories present various aspects of love at a time only a couple of generations from now in a future where real nature is gone.

The story *The California Queen Comes A-Calling*, by Pat MacEwen in Gordon Van Gelder's collection *Welcome to the Greenhouse* presents a believable, nuanced scenario of life in a new frontier after the second of two catastrophic sea level rises. Justice is delivered by a circuit judge using a paddle-wheel steamer as his courthouse.

This short list of movies includes themes of recycling people, robots with morals, resource limitation, unspecified apocalypse, and exhaustion of the Earth:

- *Soylent Green* (1973) is set in a nightmarishly crowded New York of 2022. A detective, suspecting that the murder of a top executive of the Soylent Corporation is an assassination, becomes a target himself when he discovers the true nature of the ingredient(s) of the processed foodstuff fed to the population.

- *Blade Runner* (1982), again set in a crowded future city, ultimately questions the value of humans when extremely human-like robots (may) have morals.

- *The Ballad of Narayama* (1983) is set in a poor village in a remote valley where those who reach the age of 70 are expected to leave the village and die, so that the village can continue to support itself and so the family will not be disgraced.

- *The Postman* (1997) is set in a post war world where a wandering entertainer, having escaped from a neo-fascist army, poses as a postman and sows the (false) hope that the government survived.

- *The Road* (2009) is set in an apocalyptic future. A father and son walk toward the sea, hoping doggedly to find safety, if not support. The father dies and the son must choose whether or not to join a small group that has been shadowing them.

- *Interstellar* (2014) is set in a collapsed but still struggling Earth. This film examines, with several plot twists, the search for other inhabitable worlds.

HOW MANY IS TOO MANY?

How many people can the Earth support? The question matters because:

> The results of human reproduction are no longer solely the concern of the two individuals involved, or of the larger family, or even of the nation of which they are citizens. A stage has been reached in the demographic development of the world when the rate of human reproduction in any part of the globe may directly or indirectly affect the health and welfare of the rest of the human race. It is in this sense that there is a world population problem.[187]

This was written in 1962, well over 50 years ago. Since then, the population has more than doubled from a bit above 3 billion to the current 7.4 billion.

Putting a number on carrying capacity is hard. Joel Cohen says

> The question is obviously incomplete. Support with what kind of life? With what technology? For how long? Leaving what kind of earth for the future?[188]

After nine chapters of introduction and preparation, Cohen devotes seven chapters to the discussion of carrying capacity. Since 1950 estimates of the number of people that the earth can support have ranged from 0.5 billion to 100 billion, depending largely on the standard of living chosen and the length of survival desired.[189] Many of the higher estimates assume vegetarian diets. Kingsley Davis is quoted on page 261 of Cohen as saying "... there is no country on earth in which people are satisfied with having barely enough to eat."

Standard of living, too, is not simple, for it takes into account only us humans, even though we are interrelated with all other life forms. We'd best not crowd out something vital to our survival, and there should be global buy-in for whatever standard of living is picked.

In the introductory paragraphs to Chapter 13, Cohen explicitly quashes our hope for a specific number for carrying capacity, writing:

> Estimating how many people the earth can support requires more than demographic arithmetic. ... it involves

both natural constraints that humans cannot change and do not fully understand, and human choices that are yet to be made by this and future generations. Therefore the question 'How many people can the earth support?' has no single numerical answer, now or ever.

It's incomplete to talk about carrying capacity and consider only humans. Though Cohen didn't mention it explicitly above, we share the Earth with more creatures and more kinds of creatures than have even been named. Nor can we say which ones are critical in some unforeseen way to our survival. That mandates humility and diversity when considering humans' place on the Earth.

In *Discourse on the Origin and Basis of Inequality Among Men* (1755), philosopher Jean-Jacques Rousseau wrote:

> The first man who, having enclosed a piece of ground, bethought himself of saying *This is mine*, and found people simple enough to believe him, was the real founder of civil society. From how many crimes, wars, and murders, from how many horrors and misfortunes might not any one have saved mankind, by pulling up the stakes, or filling up the ditch, and crying to his fellows: Beware of listening to this imposter; you are undone if you once forget that the fruits of the earth belong to us all, and the earth itself to nobody.

ENDNOTE

Whatever the carrying capacity, no matter how little the Earth complains, it's worthwhile to note how Shel Silverstein's book *The Giving Tree* ends. After giving herself as a place to play, as shade, as fruit, as branches and trunk, she offers this:

> "Well," said the tree, straightening herself up as much as she could,
>
> "well, an old stump *is* good for sitting and resting. Come, Boy, sit down.

Sit down and rest. And the boy did."[190]

But the tree is gone, used up, its fruit and shade and housing for birds and squirrels lost to the future. On the savanna, there was a natural understanding of overconsumption. Centuries later, births were regulated somewhat by social pressure and individual convenience, using infanticide and baby farming. Now there's war and abortion, spurts of global disease, and starvation through maldistribution and poverty.

What next? What do we see from a global, deep-time[191] point of view?

FIFTH PIECE

Plain Talk From the Earth's Point of View

I saw a man crying in a line,
and I didn't know, if he began to faint,
if I could hold him up.[192]

INTENTION

The First Piece presents that life is a gift, as if of a higher power. It reflects on the goodness of fit of human beings with the Earth and how to respond.

The Second Piece presents that humans are at the top of the intelligence chain and examines the implications of being at the top.

The Third Piece inventories many of the current environmental issues afflicting the Earth. It finds population to be a factor common to each issue.

The Fourth Piece faces the common factor, mentioning some of the ways nature and humans affect both animal and human populations.

This Fifth Piece offers plain talk about a carefully sized global population.

SOME THOUGHTS FROM THE EARLY PIECES

- The Earth's fruits are not distributed evenly or fairly. Nor are wastes discarded evenly or fairly.

- The Earth suffers resource depletion and waste generation without complaint, but depletion and waste have consequences.

- New birth and healing arise alongside destruction and defilement, though some destruction and defilements take geologic time to heal.

- Some resources do not have substitutes. Sunshine, clean air, healthy water, and land itself come easily to mind.

- The idea that discovery determines ownership disempowers the original population.

- Environmental harm is occurring at the current level of demand for food, goods, services, and waste management.

- Population growth, healthy aging, longer life spans, and a rising standard of living all increase demand.

- Technological advances do not reduce demand, they empower growth.

- Robots and automation reduce jobs.

- Even if the population fell in the next two centuries as fast as it rose in the last two, the basic shapes of Figures 2.4 and 3.3 would not change.

- We interdepend with all life. Interbeing does not increase with the addition, nor decrease with the subtraction, of people.

- Fertility rates below replacement level are happening around the world.

PLAIN TALK
PREMISE

The premise of these Five Pieces is that the Earth is a treasure currently saturated with more people than it can support in a way that's sustainable and healthy for the planet and all of Creation.

The cry at the beginning of this Fifth Piece is one man's existential fear, a fear that we all face individually. There is another existential fear, one that humans face collectively: the possibility that our lineages, our species, this Creation itself will end, perhaps by our own hands.

Women's intuition and awareness are underappreciated strengths. Though society imprints women as well as men with its urgency, enticements, and demands, women seem to naturally understand what they can directly affect—family size. Smaller families are best accomplished couple by couple. Population care is simply couples' collective response to the state of the Earth and the life they foresee for their children and all of Earth's life.

ABOUT FEAR(S)

A call for smaller families raises anxiety and fear. Growth feels positive and, being familiar, promotes feelings of aliveness, even safety. De-growth feels negative and, being unfamiliar, brings feelings of apprehension and loss. But "Fear is a feeling, not a fact."[193]

Not all fears are bad, not all strengths are good, so we face fears with respect and compassion and strengths with respect and wisdom. Why compassion for fears? Because they are the sufferings of real people, just like us. And why wisdom for strengths? Because some strengths should not be used. And why respect for both? Because they can both be powerful teachers.

Wendell Berry speaks about fears from a place of open vulnerability:

> I go among trees and sit still.
> All my stirring becomes quiet
> around me like circles on water.
> My tasks lie in their places
> where I left them, asleep like cattle.
> Then what is afraid of me comes
> and lives a while in my sight.
> What it fears in me leaves me,
> and the fear of me leaves it.
> It sings, and I hear its song.
> Then what I am afraid of comes.
> I live for a while in its sight.
> What I fear in it leaves it,
> and the fear of it leaves me.
> It sings, and I hear its song.

After days of labor,

mute in my consternations,

I hear my song at last,

and I sing it. As we sing,

the day turns, the trees move.[194]

There is no end to the list of fears, no end, even, to the categories of fears. Nor is there any end to the list of strengths or categories of strengths. Further, there is no assurance that every fear has an opposing strength, nor that every strength arises to meet a fear.[195]

When the issues of the Third and Fourth Pieces are presented as fears, the appropriate response is compassion and wisdom. To stir emotion to emphasize such issues is a concern, because an appeal to emotion can empower division and circumvent compassion and wisdom. To sow doubt and fear is to seek control.

THE ANTHROPOCENE

The declaration of a new geologic era, the Anthropocene (the Age of Humans), is science's confirmation of the moral claim made in the First and Second Pieces that humans are responsible for the fate of the Earth, that the Earth's well-being falls to us. Our effect on the Anthropocene comes from our newfound ability to make changes to life itself and our numbers. These newfound powers offer the ability to make changes that affect the far distant future, while the power of numbers is apparent in Figure 2.4. Ban Ki-moon, when Secretary General of the United Nations, said "The time has come to acknowledge that national interests are best served by acting in the global interest.[196,197] This is true, but incomplete—the health of the Earth in the Anthropocene also requires acting with deep-time awareness.

One unspoken fear of a smaller population is that progress will be reduced or slowed; that with fewer people, the future will have fewer break-throughs in science and medicine and food production and defense. These are existential fears, whether they are of an individual fearing that cure of a disease will be lost or of a species afraid it will die out. These fears are worthy of compassion for they call for an increasing maturity and under-standing of limits and of change. At its root, progress is about offering a new understanding along with a clear statement of the consequences and cautions of that understanding.

LIFE ITSELF

Joanna Macy, in her preface to *Rilke's Book of Hours* writes:

> There came a time in the middle and late 1970s when the enormity of what I was discovering as an environmental activist—especially about the widespread, long term, devastating effects of nuclear waste—broke through my defenses. I struggled simply to take in what was happening to our world, and to sustain the gaze long enough to be of use. Rilke's unwhining acceptance of the fact that, yes, a world can die, strengthened me with its straightforwardness and lack of self pity.[198]

Just as a plant can get root-bound in a pot, so the Earth can get saturated with people. Both root-bound plants and a saturated Earth are better addressed through prevention than choking. A carefully sized global population avoids choking.

The reason for caring about a saturated Earth is the same as the reason for caring about social justice: rather than thinking just about descendants of *mine*, all descendants are really descendants of *ours*, so caring for unknown current persons (social justice) is the best way to care for descendants. Herman Daly and John Cobb, Jr. write:

> Your great-great grandchild will also be the great-great grandchild of fifteen other people in the current generation, many of their identities now unknown. Presumably your great-great grandchild's well being will be as much an inheritance from each of these fifteen others as from yourself. Therefore it does not make sense for you to worry too much about your particular descendant, or to take any particular action on his or her behalf. The farther in the future is the hypothetical descendant, the greater the number of co-progenitors in the present generation, and consequently the more in the nature of a public good

is any provision made for the distant future. To the extent that you are concerned about the welfare of your descendant, you should also be concerned about the welfare of all those in the present generation from whom, for good or ill, your descendant will inherit. Thus a concern for future generations should reinforce rather than weaken the concern for present justice—contrary to what is often supposed. Although we are not all brothers and sisters in the literal sense, we are quite literally co-progenitors of each others' distant descendants.[199]

This assumes that each child's development proceeds naturally, and that includes vulnerability to inherited conditions. If, somewhere in this widening mix of ancestors, someone chooses gene manipulation to correct a problem or enhance a feature of their particular child, then the flow of natural inheritance, that is, evolution, is disturbed.

GENE MANIPULATION

Elizabeth Kolbert, in her article "Unnatural Selection", writes of Ruth Gates's work to save coral reefs. Gates is director of the Hawaii Institute of Marine Biology. There, rather than trying to restore the oceans and coral to some previous condition, she works to discover how some corals survive so those strengths can be passed on to others. Gates says:

Really what I am is a futurist. Our project is acknowledging that a future is coming where nature is no longer wholly natural.[200]

Gene manipulation is here.[201] It is not entirely comforting to know that biologists have created a new form of life in the laboratory by adding a fourth base-pair to the three that have so far built all life.[202] The biologists added two new letters to the four-letter (C, G, A, T) DNA alphabet within *E. coli* bacteria. You can think of these unnatural nucleobases as X and Y.

A recent New York Times article about the possibility of using pig organs for humans had this to say about gene manipulation:

This month, scientists gathered at the National Academy of Sciences in Washington to talk about CRISPR, a new method for editing genes. In the past couple of years, the technique has become so powerful and accessible that many experts are calling for limits on its potential uses— especially altering human embryos with changes that could be inherited by future generations. ...[203]

The UK's fertility regulator has given the green light to a treatment that will make it possible for certain endangered babies to be made from two women and a man. This new advancement in in-vitro fertilization, developed by doctors in Newcastle, is intended to treat children who would otherwise be born with certain fatal genetic diseases. The first child to be born in the UK through the new method could arrive by the end of 2017.[204]

This burgeoning ability to manipulate genes will bring more, healthier, and longer-lived people into the world than ever before. It will be championed for its clear benefits while its unforeseen consequences (such as population growth) will be unexamined until they can no longer be ignored. Genes interact with and affect each other even as an embryo develops, meaning that modifying a gene in an embryo may bring unforeseen results.[205] These may be unwelcome or even irreversible changes.

Although gene manipulation is just science's acceleration of nature's evolutionary process, science is not given the time that nature takes to sort things out. Nor is science allowed nature's indifference to suffering. Gene manipulation is a strength that sometimes should not be used, and those times are clearest in retrospect.

Modifying plant genes is different from modifying animal (human) genes. So far, GMO seeds generate sterile crops; new seeds are needed for each new crop. Genetically modified plants are created to improve crop yields by making plants that grow better in unfavorable conditions and that survive insecticides and weed killers. A carefully sized population reduces this need.

LONGEVITY

The rolling loss of reference, the rising elevator of life expectancy, and the efforts to unleash longevity will bring increasing demand for goods and services and place from a growing elder population. The transition to a carefully sized population decreases the birth rate, magnifying the social disruption of this trend toward longer life. The percentage of elders in the population will increase and the gap between younger and older could widen. Living a long life in a future where young and old are at odds would not be a blessing.

CONTRACEPTION

At the beginning of the author's epilogue to *Countdown*, Alan Weisman writes this:

> Let's suppose, however—theoretically, social objections aside—that the entire world adopted a one-child policy tomorrow. By the end of this century, we would be back to 1.6 billion, our population in 1900.
>
> That sounds incredible, but it's true if you think about it: If we stopped reproducing completely, in little more than a hundred years our population would be zero. So holding to just one offspring per family for a few generations would exponentially bring us down to size.
>
> That would reduce our numbers by three-quarters, freeing billions of acres for other species, on whose existence a functioning ecosystem—including our place in it—depends.[206]

And it would dramatically reduce the population's impact on the Earth, giving it a chance to recover in a way we might guide with some wisdom.

Though to use contraceptives is to deny life, it can be argued that denying life is not the same as ending it.[207] The issue of contraception presents two opposing fears. The fear that calls *for* contraception is population overshoot, whether it's one more child in a family or the accumulation of children worldwide. Being a fear, overshoot calls for compassion. The fear that calls *against* contraception is the fear that a life may be ended. This also needs compassion. So we're left with opposing fears, possible overshoot versus possible destruction, and the unenviable task of balancing one compassion against another.

96

Smaller families for now seem possible when both male and female contraceptives are readily available wherever desired. However, there are arguments against contraception, whether it's internally chosen or externally imposed. It is tempting to declare all externally imposed constraints as wrong, given our Western love of freedom and the experience of China and Iran, but some religions' resistance to contraception feels externally imposed, putting two significant loyalties (freedom to prevent and religious injunction) in opposition.

Wendell Berry speaks about fertility in a section of *The Art of the Commonplace* titled "'Freedom' from Fertility." He says:

> The household is the bond of marriage that is most native to it, that grows with it and gives it substantial being in the world. It is the practical condition within which husband and wife can enact devotion and loyalty to each other. The motive power of sexual love is thus joined directly to constructive work and is given communal and ecological value. ...
>
> To last, love must enflesh itself in the materiality of the world—produce food, shelter, warmth or shade, surround itself with careful acts, well-made things. ...
>
> Marriage and the care of the earth are each other's disciplines. Each makes possible the enactment of fidelity toward the other. ...[208]

This deep understanding of household, constructive work, and care is part of an essay that includes advocating restraint. Restraint has typically arisen at times and in places where resources were clearly limited and the community was in agreement on this common need. That's not the case now, for the Earth's limits are not universally acknowledged and biology remains more powerful than individual will power.

ECONOMICS

Though these Five Pieces address existential fears for humans and for the Creation, the most immediate fear for most is not existential, it's economic. For most, death is less immediately threatening than inflation or unemployment or debt.

Economics is both important and mysterious, making it the realm of the highly educated, but the authority of higher education is not immune to common sense and common decency. Every barbershop on Main Street must have had someone who foresaw the housing bubble. Every barbershop on Wall Street must have had someone who foresaw the danger in credit default swaps. When the fear of speaking up and being laughed at partners with the fear of losing out on the bubble, together they can seem irresistible, but the strength of speaking up is just as powerful, just as real, and more shocking than keeping silent. Common sense matters, and, as seen in *The Big Short* (2015), it can be profitable.

ECOLOGICAL ECONOMICS, STATIONARY ECONOMICS, SUSTAINABLE DEGROWTH

As the ones who hold the Earth's point of view, who champion, defend, and protect its being and its ability to nourish, we are challenged to develop an economic system that does not steal its fruits, or see them overused, wasted, or spoiled.

Ecological economics are not new. K. William Kapp and Karl Polanyi were writing about it in the 1940s; Kenneth Boulding and Herman Daly in the 1960s; and Brian Czech, Dennis Meadows, Donella Meadows, and Jørgen Randers, and Tim Jackson in the 2000s. Books by Tim Jackson on *Prosperity without Growth* and by Herman Daly and Joshua Farley on *Ecological Economics* lay out a path toward an economy that is not based on perpetual growth.

Nor are stationary economics new. An interview by Warren Olney with Herman Daly and John Cobb mentions John Stuart Mill writing on the steady-state economy in the late 1850s.[209] Ecological and stationary economics are not the only alternatives. Sustainable degrowth economics are being developed, published, and debated.[210] The phrase "sustainable degrowth" can be seen as either darkly comic or truly frightening, but it is neither an oxymoron nor a death sentence:

> By "degrowth", we understand a form of society and economy which aims at the well-being of all and sustains the natural basis of life. ... We are convinced that the common values of a degrowth society should be care, solidarity and cooperation. ...[211]

Tim Jackson, author of *Prosperity without Growth,* is a major figure in the movement. The fifth international conference on sustainable degrowth was held in 2016 in Budapest.[212] It's reassuring that many smart people have been thinking hard about this for nearly a decade.

JOBS

Research on various forms of a possible new economy, important as it is, is a distant kerfuffle compared to job loss. The shift to robots and automation is a big, perhaps the final, step in the race to find the lowest wage worker.

> Between 2010 and 2015, according to the International Federation of Robotics, sales of industrial robots globally went up almost 60% ...
>
> Foxconn, the company that assembles Apple products this year replaced 60,000 workers with robots.[213]

Martin Ford thoroughly assesses the effects of automation in his book *Rise of the Robots, Technology and the Threat of a Jobless Future.* After nine chapters describing the advances and implications of automation he mentions the problem with assuming that retraining will help:

> We are running up against a fundamental limit both in terms of the capabilities of the people being herded into colleges and the number of high-skill jobs that will be available for them if they manage to graduate. The problem is that the skills ladder is not really a ladder at all: it is a pyramid, and there is only so much room at the top.[214]

In his conclusion Ford notes a report by the Bureau of Labor Statistics that showed in 1998 workers put in 194 billion hours of work. A decade and a half later, after a 42 percent increase in output, workers put in that same number, 194 billion hours of work.

Shaun Sprague, the BLS economist who prepared the report, noted that 'this means that there was ultimately *no growth at all* in the number of hours worked over this 15-year period, despite the fact that the US population gained over 40 million people during that time, and despite the fact that there were thousands of new businesses established during that time.[215]

Ford's exhaustive assessment of the effects of automation ends without directly addressing population growth. He does propose:

… a combination of short term policies and longer term initiatives one of which is … a guaranteed income for all citizens.[216]

Automation and robots will migrate rapidly to undeveloped countries, bringing opportunity for a few highly skilled workers and managers, but unemployment to masses of low-skilled workers. Automation does not affect just manual assembly-line-type jobs. AI (artificial intelligence) is being introduced into the office. A Japanese insurance company has replaced 34 office workers with a computer and AI software.[217] Even AI software engineers are at risk—AI software that learns how to learn is under development and could take away some of the work done by AI experts.[218]

Replacing office workers with a computer is one thing; AI is also being put into life-form robots. Ranging from machines serving the elderly as companion animals to full-service butlers, these life-form robots are raising a discussion about equipping them with kill switches. Tenzin Priyadarshi, president and CEO of the Dalai Lama Center for Ethics and Transformative Values at MIT said

We are the closest to ever creating something that will be immortal. The challenge is that we just don't know the quality of intelligence. We can't guarantee whether this intelligence … can be used for destruction or not.[219]

How do you know a robot's intention; how do you know when it's lying?

Late in August 2016 the internet splashed forth the news that Amazon is experimenting with a reduced workweek for a small number of particular teams of people. Those in the teams will work 30 hours a week for 75 percent of full-time pay, with benefits. The reasons presented for this trial include 1) to offer a work environment with a reduced schedule but career paths, 2) to address a diverse workforce that doesn't fit a 40-hour work-week, and 3) to diminish the stigma associated with 'part-time' work.[220]

An article about this in *Fortune* adds:

> But this is about more than just one company's culture. The idea of a work week of 30 hours or less also speaks to several large-scale issues around technology and employment. More and more voices are arguing that automation is lowering overall labor demand in the economy, a trend that will only increase. A 30 hour work week is seen by some as a way to more evenly distribute the shrinking pool of labor among workers, and reduce the potential of automation to increase income inequality.[221]

This can be a start, but an even distribution of less work only addresses one side of the issue. Dropping to even a 10-hour workweek does not address a growing work force for long—a carefully sized population is still needed.

An op–ed in the *LA Times* of July 9, 2017 notes that the lack of jobs involving hard, physical work means that something needed has been lost.[222] The author cites the proliferation of hard-work reality-television shows as evidence of the appeal of this work. He says he learned more teaching at Cal State Fresno than at Stanford because the students at Cal State often worked 20 hours a week outside of school and thus had a wider range of experience and empathy.

Wendell Berry knows the centrality of work to personhood. In his book *What Are People For?* he writes:

> Good work finds the way between pride and despair. It graces with health. It heals with grace. It preserves the given so that it remains a gift. By it, we lose loneliness: we clasp the hands of those who go before us, and the hands of those who come after us; we enter the little circle of each other's arms, ...[223]

In good work we come to know our interdependence. Children with household tasks do useful work and learn valuable life-discipline. Elders' lives remain vital when they volunteer, knitting blankets and wraps, sorting and organizing donations, cleaning beaches, waterways and neighborhoods, protesting pollution and corruption. These activities are the micro-economies of households, the mini-economies of communities.

PREDATION

The predation with the greatest current impact on population is humans waging war on humans. This predation is apparent in the sporadic genocides and ongoing territorial and religious disputes. War, however, cannot be used as a means of population care, for a significant reduction in a population of 7.4 billion would involve nuclear war, and nuclear war poisons the Earth for everything.

Joe Scarborough, on his *Morning Joe* program, said

> Several months ago, a foreign policy expert on the international level went to advise Donald Trump. And three times [Trump] asked about the use of nuclear weapons. Three times, he asked at one point if we had them why can't we use them, ...[224]

One can read Trump's question as a hint that we could reduce some of these weapons. But that may not be what he meant.

WATER

Water is central to life. Currently, water supplies are threatened not only for industry and farming, but for all life. Reclaimed water is used for irrigation along roads, and it may need to be used for people. Could it be that Malthus was right, but about healthy water rather than food?

Climate change will alter the distribution of arid and verdant lands as historic patterns of rainfall no longer hold. There's no reason to believe that the newly rainy areas will align with good, available soil, or that they will remain aligned anywhere at all. If rainy areas develop a habit of moving around, that is called migratory food production. If rain falls where the soil is bad or unavailable and drought comes where the soil is good, that is called lose–lose.

RAISING A LOW TOTAL FERTILITY RATE (TFR)

Mei Fong's book *One China* reports that now that small families have been established, only a modest percentage of families take the opportunity to have more children. She writes:

> After over three decades of the one-child policy, the Communist Party has finally taken steps to end it, only to find to its dismay that many middle-class Chinese don't want more than one child.
>
> The take up has been far below even the most pessimistic projections. Only a tenth of eligible couples applied for permission to have a second child.[225]

Pat Buchanan focused on the West in his book *The Death of the West*, which comes to a similar conclusion about many Western nations where the trend has been toward smaller families. A wider, global view would also lament the below replacement TFRs of places like Hong Kong, South Korea, Japan, Taiwan, and Singapore.

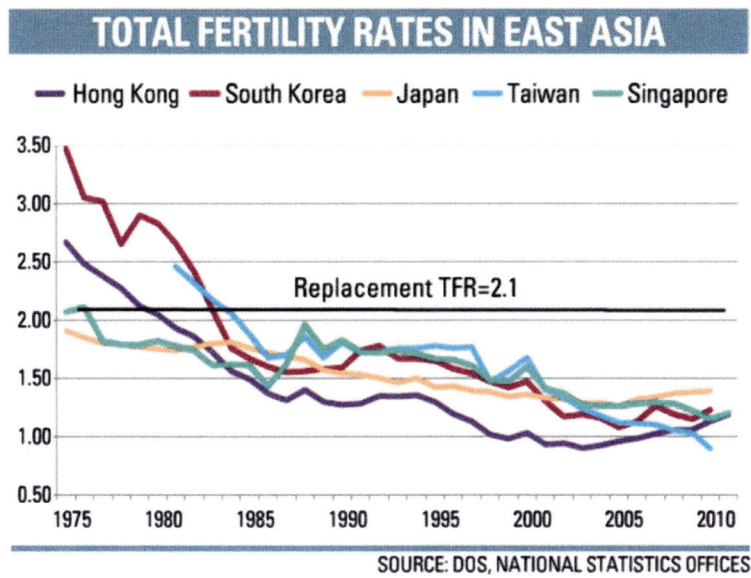

Figure 5.1

Rather than being a problem, a shrinking population can be seen as an intelligent, appropriate, even healthy response to places as crowded as Hong Kong (7.3 mil @ 6,300/sqkm), Tokyo (13.5 mil @ 6,200/sqkm), Singapore (5.1 mil @ 7,100/sqkm), or Lagos (16 mil @ 13,700/sqkm).[226]

Japan has stopped having enough babies to maintain its current population (a population pyramid for Japan is shown in Figure 2.3b). Japan is not alone. Germany, for instance, has a similar pyramid, and East Asia may soon follow.

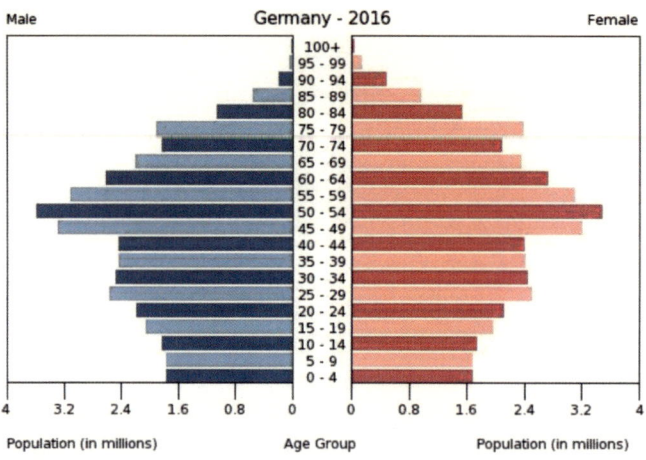

Figure 5.2[227]

Japan and Germany are just two of the countries pioneering this shift. They are testing and learning what works and what doesn't when the population pyramid is upended. As more and more countries go through this transition from growth to degrowth, wisdom and compassion become the strengths that ensure that households are preserved, nourished, and respected for everyone.

Will low TFRs ever climb back up to replacement level? Yes, as soon as there is wild space a bicycle's ride from home, as soon as everyone who wants to can find a seat on the commuter train or space on the freeway, as soon as calamity is down in the daily news, as soon as dignified work is available to all. In an interview with Josephine Ferorelli (a climate justice activist) and Meghan Kallman (a sociologist and environmentalist) for NPR's *All Things Considered*, Jennifer Ludden closes the report with this about Ferorelli: Every day, she says she looks for some clue that the future will feel safe enough to have a baby.[228]

GLOBAL COMMONS

Currently we may think of *sharing* in personal terms—sharing information, for instance, using social media, or sharing time and resources with friends and the less fortunate. A broader view of sharing, one from Earth's point of view, involves all of Earth's life and inter-dependencies. It suggests a global commons approach to things that affect the whole Earth for deep time.

The electromagnetic frequency spectrum is a form of global common that we all share and use. The communication technique called 5G will reshape the way we use mobile devices. It will deliver self-driving cars and smart cities, guide drones, and even affect the way content gets to our homes.[229] Things such as outer space, sunlight, clean air, healthy water, land, biodiversity, and even wild space could well be considered as finite global commons. But we do not seem ready to do this because, again, we don't universally recognize them as global, finite, and without substitute.

ENDNOTES

I begin these endnotes with great thanks and a quote from Carlos Castaneda:

> Only if one loves this Earth with unbending passion can one release one's sadness... This lovely being, which is alive to its last recesses, and understands every feeling, soothed me, it cured me of my pains, and finally, when I had fully understood my love for it, it taught me freedom.[230]

SUPPOSE...

As our distant ancestors respected the constraint of limited food by consciously limiting population, suppose we respected the constraint of a limited Earth by avoiding families larger, collectively, than the Earth can support. After all, it's easier now. Our distant ancestors had to deal with hunger, predation, disease, exposure, and, later, great shame. They used infanticide where we can use prevention.

Having honored gratitude, service, and responsibility; having considered population size, impact, and purpose; having inventoried issues and identified their common factor; having described history's population care; and having mulled over both immediate and deep-future concerns; there is still much more. Infinite service and infinite responsibility are a matter of making wise choices, choices that honor a finite Earth and our ability to affect all of its future. This is not inherently good or bad, easy or hard, but it requires a full-bodied attention. Like doing the dishes, raking the yard, changing the oil, and planning a vacation, gratitude, service and responsibility are part of life.

BIBLIOGRAPHY

- Barker, K. (Ed.). (1999). *NASB Study Bible.* Grand Rapids, MI: Zondervan.
- Barrows, A & Macy, J. (Trans.). (1996). *Rilke's Book of Hours, Love Poems to God.* New York, NY: Riverhead Books.
- Baum, G. (1990). *The Rabbi With A Reputation.* Los Angeles, CA: Los Angeles Times (pre-1997 Fulltext).
- Berry, T. (1990). *The Dream Of The Earth.* San Francisco, CA: Sierra Club Books.
- Berry, W. (1977, 1996). *The Unsettling Of America, Culture & Agriculture.* San Francisco, CA: Sierra Club Books.
- Berry, W. (1981). *The Gift Of Good Land. Further Essays Cultural And Agricultural.* New York, NY: North Point Press.
- Berry, W. (1998). *A Timbered Choir.* Berkeley, CA: Counterpoint Press.
- Berry, W. (2002). *The Art Of The Commonplace. The Agrarian Essays Of Wendell Berry.* Berkeley, CA: Counterpoint.
- Berry, W. (1990, 2010). *What Are People For? Essays.* Berkeley, CA: Counterpoint.
- Biello, D. (2012). *Walking The Line: How To Identify Safe Limits For Human Impacts On The Planet.* http://www.scientificamerican.com/article/do-planetary-boundaries-help-humanity-manage-environ-mental-impacts/.
- Biello, D. (2010). *If The World Is Going To Hell, Why Are Humans Doing So Well?* http://blogs.scien-tificamerican.com/observations/2010/09/01/if-the-world-is-going-to-hell-why-are-humans-doing-so-well/.
- Birdsall, N., Kelley, A. C., & Sinding, S. W. (Eds.). (2001, 2003). *Population Matters. Demographic Change, Economic Growth, And Poverty In The Developing World.* Oxford, UK: Oxford University Press.
- Bly, R. (1990). *Iron John, A Book About Men.* Reading, MA: Addison-Wesley Publishing Company.
- Brooks, D. (2015). *The Structure Of Gratitude.* http://nyti.ms/1IF31is.

- Brown, D. (1970). *Bury My Heart At Wounded Knee. An Indian History Of The American West.* New York, NY: St. Martin's Press.
- Brown, L. R., Gardner, G., Halweil, B. (1999). *Beyond Malthus, Nineteen Dimensions Of The Population Challenge.* New York, London: W. W. Norton & Company.
- Brown, L. R., Kane, H. (1994). *Full House, Reassessing The Earth's Population Carrying Capacity.* New York, London: W. W. Norton & Co.
- Buchanan, P. J. (2002). *The Death Of The West. How Dying Populations And Immigrant Invasions Imperil Our Country and Civilization.* New York, NY: St. Martin's Press.
- Bush, M. B. (1997). *Ecology Of A Changing Planet.* Upper Saddle River, NJ: Prentice Hall.
- Castaneda, C. (1974). *Tales of Power.* New York, NY: Simon and Schuster.
- Cipolla, C. M. (1978, Seventh Edition). *The Economic History Of World Population.* New York, NY: Penguin.
- Cohen, J. (1995). *How Many People Can the Earth Support?* New York, NY: W. W. Norton & Co.
- Coward, H. & Maguire, D. (Eds.). (2000). *Visions Of A New Earth. Religious Perspectives On Population, Consumption, And Ecology.* Albany, NY: State University of New York Press.
- Czech, B. (2000). *Shoveling Fuel For A Runaway Train, Errant Economists, shameful spenders, and a plan to stop them all.* Berkeley, CA: University of California Press.
- Daly, H. & Cobb, J. (1989). *For The Common Good, Redirecting The Economy Toward Community, The Environment, And A Sustainable Future.* Boston, MA: Beacon Press.
- Daum, M. (2015). *Selfish, Shallow, And Self-Absorbed. Sixteen Writers On The Decision NOT To Have Kids.* New York, NY: Picador.
- DeFries, R., (2014). *The Big Ratchet. How Humanity Thrives In The Face Of Natural Crises.* New York, NY: Basic Books.
- Dorn, H., 1962, in Cox, George W., ed. (1969). *Readings in conservation ecology.* New York, NY: Appleton-Century-Crofts. pg274.

- Efal, R., (2015). *NATIVE AMERICAN PRE–RETREAT INFORMATION.* Zenpeacemakers.org
- Ehrlich, P., & Ehrlich, A. (1990). *The Population Explosion.* New York, NY: Simon & Schuster.
- Fong, M. (2016). *One Child, The Story Of China's Most Radical Experiment.* Boston, MA & New York, NY: Houghton Mifflin Harcourt.
- Ford, M. (2015). *Rise of the Robots, Technology and the Threat of a Jobless Future.* New York, NY: Basic Books.
- Gallant, R. A. (1990). *The Peopling of Planet Earth. Human Population Growth Through the Ages.* New York, NY: Macmillan Publishing Co.
- Gever, J., Kaufmann, R., Skole, D., & Vorosmarty, C. (1986). *Beyond Oil. The Threat to Food and Fuel in the Coming Decades.* Cambridge, MA: Ballinger Publishing Company.
- *Green Bible, The.* NRSV, (2008). New York, NY: HarperCollins Publishers.
- Glover, J. (1990). *Causing Death and Saving Lives.* London, England: Penguin Books Ltd.
- Haidt, J. (2012). *The Righteous Mind. Why Good People Are Divided By Politics And Religion.* New York, NY: Pantheon Books.
- Hanh, T. N. (2008). *The World We Have, A Buddhist Approach to Peace And Ecology*, Berkeley, CA: Parallax Press.
- Hawken, P. (2007). *Blessed Unrest, How The Largest Movement In The World Came Into Being And Why No One Saw It Coming.* New York, NY: the Penguin Group.
- Hecht, J. M. (2013). *Stay, A History Of Suicide And The Philosophies Against It.* New Haven, CT & London: Yale University Press
- Jackson, T. (2009). *Prosperity Without Growth, Economics for a Finite Planet.* United Kingdom: earthscan.
- Jamieson, D., & Nadzam, B. (2015). *Love In The Anthropocene.* New York, NY & London, England: OR Books.
- Kelly, M. & J. (1992). *One Hundred Graces.* New York, NY: Bell Tower.
- Kohl, M. (1979). *Infanticide and the Value of Life* New York, NY: Prometheus Books. pgs61-75.

- Loori, J. D. (2007). *Teachings Of The Earth*. Boston, MA & London, UK: Shambhala.
- Macy, J. (2007). *World As Lover, World As Self.* Berkeley, CA: Parallax Press.
- Macy, J., Johnstone, C. (2012). *Active Hope. How to Face the Mess We're in without Going Crazy*. Novato, CA: New World Library.
- McFague, S. (1993). *The Body Of God, An Ecological Theology*. Minneapolis, MN: Fortress Press.
- Meadows, D. H., Meadows, D. L., & Randers, J. (1992). *Beyond The Limits, Confronting global collapse, envisioning a sustainable future*. Post Mills, VT: Chelsea Green Publishing Co.
- Merwin, W. (1988). *Migration: New & Selected Poems*. Port Townsend, WA: Copper Canyon Press.
- Miyazaki, H. (2001). *Spirited Away*. Studio Ghibli Production: Buena Vista Home Entertainment: Burbank, CA.
- Neihardt, J. G. (Flaming Rainbow). (1932, preface 1961). *Black Elk Speaks. Being the Life Story of a Holy Man of the Oglala Sioux*. New York, NY: Morrow (1932).
- Nerburn, K., & Mengelkoch, L. (Eds.). (1991). *Native American Wisdom*. Novato, CA: The Wisdom Collection, New World Library.
- Newcomb, S. (2008). *Pagans in the Promised Land, Decoding the Doctrine of Christian Discovery*. Golden, CO: Fulcrum Publishing.
- Norris, G. (1992). *Sharing Silence*. New York, NY: Bell Tower Books.
- O'Rourke, P. J. (1994). *All The Trouble In The World: The Lighter Side of Overpopulation, Famine, Ecological Disaster, Ethnic Hatred, Plague, and Poverty*. New York, NY: The Atlantic Monthly Press.
- Perrini, S. (2012). *Baby Farmers of the 19th Century, Women Who Kill*. Published by Goldmineguides.com.
- Porter, A. (2006). *Living Things, Collected Poems*. Hanover, NH: Zoland Books, An Imprint of Steerforth Press.
- Pullinger, M. (2014). *Working time reduction policy in a sustainable economy: Criteria and options for its design*. Elsevier B.V. http://dx.doi.org/10.1016/j.ecolecon.2014.04.009

- Reining, P. (1979). *Challenging Desertification In West Africa*. Athens, Ohio: Ohio University Center for International Studies, Africa Program, 1980.
- Rilke, R. (1992). *Duino Elegies*. (D. Young, Trans.). New York, NY: W.W. Norton & Co., Inc.
- Rilke, R. (1997). *Rilke's Book of Hours. Love Poems To God*. (A. Barrows & J. Macy, Trans.). New York, NY: Riverhead Books, Berkeley Publishing Group.
- Rockstrom, J. & Klum, M. (2015). *Big World Small Planet*. New Haven, CT: Yale University Press.
- Rumi, M. (2004). *The Essential Rumi. New Expanded Edition*. (C. Barks, R. Nicholson, A. Arberry, & J. Moyne, Trans.). New York, NY: HarperCollins Publishers, Inc.
- Schor, J. B. & Taylor, B. (Eds). (2002). *Sustainable Planet, Solutions for the Twenty-first Century*. Boston, MA: Beacon Press.
- Scranton, R. (2015). *Learning to Die in the Anthropocene, Reflections on the End of a Civilization*. San Francisco, CA: City Lights Books.
- Silver, N. (2012). *The Signal and the Noise, Why So Many Predictions Fail – But Some Don't*. New York, NY: The Penguin Press.
- Silverstein, S. (1964). *The Giving Tree*. New York, NY: Harper & Row, Publishers.
- Simon, J. (1996). *The Ultimate Resource 2*. Princeton, NJ: Princeton University Press.
- Simon, J. (1999). *Hoodwinking the Nation*. New Brunswick, NJ: Transaction Publishers.
- Spikins, P. (2015). *How Compassion Made us Human: An Archeology of Stone Age Sentiment*. South Yorkshire S70 2AS, England: Pen and Sword Books Ltd.
- Stafford, W. (2014). *Ask Me*. Minneapolis, MN: Graywolf Press.
- Tisdale, S. (2010). https://tricycle.org/magazine/if-there-nothing-lose/.
- Van Gelder, G. (Ed.). (2011). *Welcome To The Greenhouse*. New York, NY: OR Books.
- Vaughan-Lee, L. (Ed.). (2013). *Spiritual Ecology, The Cry Of The Earth*. Point Reyes, CA: The Golden Sufi Center.

- Weisman, A. (2013). *Countdown, Our last, best hope for a future on earth?*. New York, NY, Boston, MA, London, UK: Little, Brown & Company.
- Whitman, W. (1855). *Leaves of Grass, A Song of the Rolling Earth*. Brooklyn, NY: Fulton Street printing shop.
- Zeaman, J. (2002). *Overpopulation*. New York, NY, Toronto, CN, London, UK, Auckland, NZ, Sydney, AUS, Mexico City, MEX, New Delhi, India, Hong Kong, Danbury, CT: Franklin Watts, A Division of Scholastic.
- Zubrow, Ezra B. W. (1975). *Prehistoric Carrying Capacity: A Model*. Menlo Park, CA: Cummings Publishing Company.

REFERENCES

1 Baum, G. (1990). *The Rabbi With A Reputation.* Los Angeles, CA: Los Angeles Times (pre-1997 Fulltext).

2 B.S. in Aerospace Engineering, with distinction, University of Kansas, 1962.

3 The bibliography itself, although I agree with Czeslaw Milosz who said: "I have read many books, but to place all those volumes on top of one another and stand on them would not add a cubit to my stature. …."

4 Roshi Wendy Egyoku Nakao, Zen Center of Los Angeles, circa 2015.

5 *Green Bible, The.* NRSV, (2008). New York, NY: HarperCollins Publishers

6 http://www.humanecologyreview.org/pastissues/her71/71abruzzi.pdf. Accessed July 17, 2017.

Note that as direct a statement of the holiness of Creation as it is, some feel it was not written by Chief Seattle. To find various versions of this speech and the controversy around them, use the link above or do an internet search for 'Chief Seattle'.

7 Neihardt, J. G. (Flaming Rainbow). (1932, preface 1961). *Black Elk Speaks. Being the Life Story of a Holy Man of the Oglala Sioux.* New York, NY: Morrow (1932).

8 Nerburn, K., & Mengelkoch, L. (Eds.). (1991). *Native American Wisdom.* Novato, CA: The Wisdom Collection, New World Library. pg31.

9 Ibid. pg43.

10 Rumi, M. (2004). *The Essential Rumi. New Expanded Edition.* (C. Barks, R. Nicholson, A. Arberry, & J. Moyne, Trans.). New York, NY: HarperCollins Publishers, Inc.

11 Rilke, R., poem II,7 pg111 of *Rilke's Book Of Hours,* Rilke, R. (1997). *Rilke's Book of Hours. Love Poems To God.* (A. Barrows & J. Macy, Trans.). New York, NY: Riverhead Books, Berkeley Publishing Group.

12 Whitman, W. (1855). *Leaves of Grass, A Song of the Rolling Earth.* Brooklyn, NY: Fulton Street printing shop.

13 Macy, J. (2007). *World As Lover, World As Self.* Berkeley, CA: Parallax Press. pg75.

14 Stafford, W. (2014). *Ask Me.* Minneapolis, MN: Graywolf Press.

15 The Green Bible, pg I-101.

16 ibid, pg I-103

17 ibid, pg I-111

18 See Matthew, Ch 22,v34-40.

19 McFague, S. (1993). *The Body Of God, An Ecological Theology.* Minneapolis, MN: Fortress Press. pg103.

20 Berry, W. (1977, 1996). *The Unsettling Of America, Culture & Agriculture.* San Francisco, CA: Sierra Club Books.. pg97.

21 http://www.achievement.org/autodoc/page/rid0int-5. This link was broken some time before July 17, 2017.

22 http://www.beliefnet.com/Inspiration/2009/07/Famous-Astronaut-Quotes.aspx?p=9. Accessed July 17, 2017

23 http://www.bing.com/images/search?q=edgar+mitchell+quotes+earth&id=4FA13889D522BD86EF1C9A0ED650EDAF-425F2FA2&FORM=IQFRBA#view=detail&id=4FA13889D522B-D86EF1C9A0ED650EDAF425F2FA2&selectedIndex=0. Accessed July 17, 2017.

24 McFague, S. (1993). *The Body Of God, An Ecological Theology.* Minneapolis, MN: Fortress Press. pg130.

25 Roshi Egyoku Nakao in the July-Sept 2016 issue of the Zen Center of Los Angeles Waterwheel.

26 Kelly, M. & J. (1992). *One Hundred Graces*. New York, NY: Bell Tower. pg12.

27 The January/February 2017 issue of Sierra, the Sierra Club magazine, pg32.

28 https://www.poetryfoundation.org/poems/44259/after-apple-picking.

29 Macy, J. (2007). *World As Lover, World As Self*. Berkeley, CA: Parallax Press. pg77.

30 Merwin, W. (1988). *Migration: New & Selected Poems*. Port Townsend, WA: Copper Canyon Press.

31 https://www.nytimes.com/2015/07/28/opinion/david-brooks-the-structure-of-gratitude.html?smid=pl-share. Accessed July 18, 2017.

32 Sallie Jiko Tisdale, As If There is Nothing to Lose. https://tricycle.org/magazine/if-there-nothing-lose/. Accessed July 18, 2017.

33 http://www.nytimes.com/2015/07/28/opinion/david-brooks-the-structure-of-gratitude.html?_r=0. Accessed July 18, 2017.

34 http://www.nytimes.com/2016/07/08/opinion/the-power-of-altruism.html. Accessed July 18, 2017.

35 Rilke, R. (1997). *Rilke's Book of Hours. Love Poems To God*. (A. Barrows & J. Macy, Trans.). New York, NY: Riverhead Books, Berkeley Publishing Group. poem I,36 pg74.

36 The Writer's Almanac for May 17, 2015. The Writer's Almanac is produced by Prairie Home Productions and presented by American Public Media. Copyright 2015 American Public Media 480 Cedar Street, Saint Paul, MN 55101.

37 McFague, S. (1993). *The Body Of God, An Ecological Theology*. Minneapolis, MN: Fortress Press. pg109.

38 Porter, A. (2006). *Living Things, Collected Poems*. Hanover, NH: Zoland Books, An Imprint of Steerforth Press. pg94.

39 Genesis 2:15 says The Lord God took man and put him in the Garden of Eden to till it and keep it.

40 See Howard Gardner's Nine Types of Intelligence at http://sky-view.vansd.org/lschmidt/Projects/The%20Nine%20Types%20of%20 Intelligence.htm. Accessed July 18, 2017.

41 DeFries, R., (2014). *The Big Ratchet. How Humanity Thrives In The Face Of Natural Crises.* New York, NY: Basic Books. pg81

42 http://www.motherjones.com/environment/2010/05/popula-tion-growth-india-vatican/. Accessed July 18, 2017.

43 http://www.newgeography.com/content/002591-looking-new-demog-raphy. Accessed July 18, 2017.

44 Cohen, J. (1995). *How Many People Can the Earth Support?* New York, NY: W. W. Norton & Co. pg 46.

45 http://web1.cnre.vt.edu/lsg/3104/Overpop.%20FINAL/800px-Dtm_ pyramids.png. Accessed July 18, 2017.

46 https://www.cia.gov/library/publications/resources/the-world-fact-book/geos/ni.html. Accessed July 18, 2017.

47 https://www.cia.gov/library/publications/resources/the-world-fact-book/geos/ja.html. Accessed Jul 18, 2017.

48 http://cdn.zmescience.com/wp-content/uploads/2014/10/world_popu-lation_1050_to_2050.jpg. Accessed July 18, 2017.

49 https://www.bing.com/images/search?view=detailV2&ccid=brd9OIe-H&id=D6637D01707413D61F1A53671E42816C190739DE&thid=OIP. brd9OIeHLOFhFCHHga5c6AEsDM&q=world+population+growth&-simid=607991079597509100&selectedIndex=20&ajaxhist=0.

50 Bush, M. B. (1997). *Ecology Of A Changing Planet.* Upper Saddle River, NJ: Prentice Hall. Figure 13.2 pg197.

51 Cipolla, C. M. (1978, Seventh Edition). *The Economic History Of World Population.* New York, NY: Penguin. pg101.

52 DeFries, R., (2014). *The Big Ratchet. How Humanity Thrives In The Face Of Natural Crises.* New York, NY: Basic Books. pg15.

53 Berry, W. (2002). *The Art Of The Commonplace. The Agrarian Essays Of Wendell Berry.* Berkeley, CA: Counterpoint. pg94.

54 Cipolla, C. M. (1978, Seventh Edition). *The Economic History Of World Population.* New York, NY: Penguin. Preface-pg13; Ch1:pg34; Ch 6.

55 Cipolla, C. M. (1978, Seventh Edition). *The Economic History Of World Population.* New York, NY: Penguin. Ch6:pg136.

56 American Heritage® Dictionary of the English Language, Fifth Edition; Collins English Dictionary – Complete and Unabridged, 12th Edition 2014; Random House Kernerman Webster's College Dictionary, © 2010 K Dictionaries Ltd. Copyright 2005, 1997, 1991; as mentioned by http://www.thefreedictionary.com/stature.

57 Cipolla, C. M. (1978, Seventh Edition). *The Economic History Of World Population.* New York, NY: Penguin. Ch5:pg126.

58 #9 in the Indian Code of Ethics offered to retreat participants in the first Bearing Witness Retreat at Pine Ridge Reservation, SD, August, 2015. See zenpeacemakers.org.

59 Loori, J. D. (2007). *Teachings Of The Earth.* Boston, MA & London, UK: Shambhala. pg16.

60 Berry, W. (1998). *A Timbered Choir: the Sabbath Poems.* Berkeley, CA 94710. Counterpoint. pg49.

61 DeFries, R., (2014). *The Big Ratchet. How Humanity Thrives In The Face Of Natural Crises.* New York, NY: Basic Books. pg3.

62 Rilke, R. (1997). *Rilke's Book of Hours. Love Poems To God.* (A. Barrows & J. Macy, Trans.). New York, NY: Riverhead Books, Berkeley Publishing Group. II, 25.

63 Berry, W. (1977). *The Unsettling of America.* San Francisco, CA, 94105: Sierra Club Books in conjunction with Counterpoint. pg7.

64 Adapted from *Ownership of Things*, by the author, Nov 2009.

[65] As of Sep 30, 2014.

[66] Speaking of sea level rise, one could argue that God's rainbow promise (Genesis 9:11-17) that He would not again wipe out the Earth with a flood suggests that sea level rise is man-made, but I won't take time to make that argument here.

[67] http://www.nytimes.com/2016/02/13/science/two-thirds-of-the-world-faces-severe-water-shortages.html?_r=0. Accessed July 24, 2017.

[68] https://en.wikipedia.org/wiki/Three_Mile_Island_accident. Accessed July 24, 2017. and https://en.wikipedia.org/wiki/Chernobyl_disaster. Accessed July 24, 2017. and https://en.wikipedia.org/wiki/Fukushima_Daiichi_nuclear_disaster. Accessed July 24, 2017.

[69] http://www.bing.com/videos/search?q=charmaine+white+face&view=-detail&mid=154648A40A67B893E1A1154648A40A67B893E1A1&-FORM=VIRE. Accessed July 24, 2017.

[70] https://en.wikipedia.org/wiki/Yucca_Mountain_nuclear_waste_repository. Accessed July 24, 2017.

[71] Perhaps this natural adaptation will allow biologists to develop a genetic mutation which protects space-travellers against radiation on long spaceflights.

[72] http://content.time.com/time/health/article/0,8599,2067562,00.html. Accessed July 24, 2017.

[73] http://www.euronews.com/2016/11/28/chernobyl-site-sealed-with-massive-steel-shield. Accessed July 24, 2017.

[74] http://www.huffingtonpost.com/entry/bikini-atoll-radiation-resettlement_us_5757cf4ee4b08f74f6c09fb4. Accessed July 24, 2017. and http://www.pnas.org/content/113/25/6833.full. Accessed July 24, 2017.

[75] Page 40 of the January/February 2017 issue of Westways Magazine.

[76] Cipolla, C. M. (1978, Seventh Edition). *The Economic History Of World Population*. New York, NY: Penguin. Ch1.

77 Macy, J., Johnstone, C. (2012). *Active Hope. How to Face the Mess We're in without Going Crazy*. Novato, CA: New World Library. Figure 5, pg90.

78 Weisman, A. (2013). *Countdown, Our last, best hope for a future on earth?*. New York, NY, Boston, MA, London, UK: Little, Brown & Company. Ch17, pg409.

79 http://fosterfarms.com/. Accessed July 24, 2017. and https://www.farmerjohn.com/. Accessed July 24, 2017.

80 https://en.wikipedia.org/wiki/Dog_breeding. Accessed July 24, 2017.

81 http://www.fgc.ca.gov/. Accessed July 24, 2017. and https://www.wcb.ca.gov/Home/About. Accessed July 24, 2017.

82 http://www.nytimes.com/2014/08/06/business/economy/population-curbs-as-a-means-to-cut-carbon-emissions.html?emc=eta1&_r=1. Accessed July 24, 2017.

83 www.worldwatch.org/nine-population-strategies-stop-short-9-billion. Accessed July 24, 2017.

84 Simon, J. (1996). *The Ultimate Resource 2*. Princeton, NJ: Princeton University Press, and Simon, J. (1999). *Hoodwinking the Nation*. New Brunswick, NJ: Transaction Publishers. and http://www.juliansimon.org/writings/Norton/. Accessed July 24, 2017.

85 Buchanan, P. J. (2002). *The Death Of The West. How Dying Populations And Immigrant Invasions Imperil Our Country and Civilization*. New York, NY: St. Martin's Press.

86 O'Rourke, P. J. (1994). *All the Trouble in the World*. New York, NY: The Atlantic Monthly Press.

87 Biello, D. (2010). *If The World Is Going To Hell, Why Are Humans Doing So Well?* http://blogs.scientificamerican.com/observations/2010/09/01/if-the-world-is-going-to-hell-why-are-humans-doing-so-well/. Accessed July 24, 2017.

[88] The source of the data for Figure 2.1 is unknown. The data for Figures 3.2, 3.3, and 3.4 is from Appendix 2 of Cohen's book *How Many People Can The Earth Support?*

[89] https://en.wikipedia.org/wiki/Dating_creation. Accessed July 24, 2017.

[90] Cohen, J. (1995). *How Many People Can the Earth Support?*. New York, NY: W. W. Norton & Company, Inc.

[91] The source for Figures 3.2, 3.3, and 3.4 is Appendix 2 of Cohen's book *How Many People Can The Earth Support?*

[92] Cipolla, C. M. (1978, Seventh Edition). *The Economic History Of World Population*. New York, NY: Penguin. Figure 11, pg11.

[93] Imagine replacing every person in the checkout line with 4 people, every car on the freeway with 4 cars.

[94] http://www.ecology.com/2011/09/18/ecological-impact-industrial-revolution/. Accessed July 24, 2017.

[95] Coward, H. & Maguire, D. (Eds.). (2000). *Visions Of A New Earth. Religious Perspectives On Population, Consumption, And Ecology*. Albany, NY: State University of New York Press.

[96] http://faculty.wwu.edu/gmyers/esssa/Hardin.html. Accessed July 24, 2017.

[97] Spirited Away by Miyazaki. A coming of age tale about a young Asian girl. She mistakenly befriends No-Face, a spirit who 'eats' anything presented, ultimately growing to a threatening size.

[98] Pullinger, M. (2014). *Working time reduction policy in a sustainable economy: Criteria and options for its design*. Elsevier B.V. http://dx.doi.org/10.1016/j.ecolecon.2014.04.009. Though Pullinger's article mainly addresses voluntary per capita consumption to reduce the environmental impacts of the global economy, it's not a far stretch to see working time reductions (job sharing) used to bring 'full' employment to a shortened work week.

99 McFague, S. (1993). *The Body Of God, An Ecological Theology*. Minneapolis, MN: Fortress Press.

100 http://www.nytimes.com/roomfordebate/2015/06/08/is-overpopulation-a-legitimate-threat-to-humanity-and-the-planet/paul-ehrlichs-population-bomb-argument-was-right. Accessed July 24, 2017.

101 http://www.nytimes.com/roomfordebate/2015/06/08/is-overpopulation-a-legitimate-threat-to-humanity-and-the-planet/the-violent-side-effect-to-high-fertility-rates. Accessed July 24, 2017.

102 http://www.nytimes.com/roomfordebate/2015/06/08/is-overpopulation-a-legitimate-threat-to-humanity-and-the-planet/empower-women-for-the-health-of-the-planet. Accessed July 24, 2017.

103 http://www.nytimes.com/roomfordebate/2015/06/08/is-overpopulation-a-legitimate-threat-to-humanity-and-the-planet/its-not-a-numbers-problem. Accessed July 24, 2017.

104 http://www.nytimes.com/roomfordebate/2015/06/08/is-overpopulation-a-legitimate-threat-to-humanity-and-the-planet/overconsumption-is-a-grave-threat-to-humanity. Accessed July 24, 2017.

105 http://www.prb.org/Publications/Media-Guides/2012/unmet-need-factsheet.aspx. Accessed July 24, 2017.

106 http://www.nytimes.com/roomfordebate/2015/06/08/is-overpopulation-a-legitimate-threat-to-humanity-and-the-planet/asia-must-build-a-less-wasteful-economy. Accessed July 24, 2017.

107 Kubler-Ross's books include: *On Grief and Grieving*; *Living With Death and Dying*; *Death is of Vital Importance*; and *On Death and Dying*.

108 Scranton, R. (2015). *Learning to Die in the Anthropocene, Reflections on the End of a Civilization*. San Francisco, CA: City Lights Books.

109 Rilke, R. (1997). *Rilke's Book of Hours. Love Poems To God.* (A. Barrows & J. Macy, Trans.). New York, NY: Riverhead Books, Berkeley Publishing Group. and Berry, W. (1977). *The Unsettling of America*. San Francisco, CA, 94105: Sierra Club Books in conjunction with Counterpoint.

[110] Evolution with a small 'e'. For instance, the evolution of bacteria and viruses.

[111] http://www.livescience.com/9761-10-animals-tools.html. Accessed July 19, 2017.

[112] Rockstrom, J. & Klum, M. (2015). *Big World Small Planet*. New Haven, CT: Yale University Press. pg32.

[113] DeFries, R., (2014). *The Big Ratchet. How Humanity Thrives In The Face Of Natural Crises*. New York, NY: Basic Books. pgs3-4 & 13-14.

[114] ibid. pgs7 & 13.

[115] https://www.britannica.com/event/Great-Leap-Forward. Accessed July 19, 2017.

[116] DeFries, R., (2014). *The Big Ratchet. How Humanity Thrives In The Face Of Natural Crises*. New York, NY: Basic Books. pg7.

[117] http://www.statisticbrain.com/world-hunger-statistics/. Accessed July 19, 2017.

[118] http://www.nytimes.com/2015/05/15/business/bird-flu-outbreak-chicken-farmers.html. Accessed July 19, 2017.

[119] http://www.msn.com/en-us/health/medical/bill-gates-warns-world-vulnerable-to-deadly-epidemic-in-next-decade/ar-BBxJ6kO?O-CID=ansmsnnews11. This link was broken before July 19, 2007.

[120] https://en.m.wikipedia.org/wiki/Natural_disaster. Accessed July 19,2017.

[121] http://static1.squarespace.com/static/559d276fe4b0a65e-c3938057/t/55df34f2e4b08e5b72c24ede/1440691442499/Gender-and-the-climate-change-agenda-212.pdf. Accessed July 19, 2017.

[122] http://www.politico.com/magazine/story/2016/03/what-works-miami-beach-sea-level-rise-213731#ixzz42vZHP5wz. Accessed July 21, 2017.

[123] http://www.explorebiology.com/documents/LE/LabPopulationControls2008.pdf. Accessed July 21, 2007.

[124] http://en.wikipedia.org/wiki/Wolves_and_moose_on_Isle_Royale. Accessed July 21, 2017.

[125] http://www.mtu.edu/news/stories/2016/april/two-wolves-remain-isle-royale.html. Accessed July 21, 2017.

[126] http://www.nasa.gov/directorates/spacetech/home/feature_3d_food. html#.V6OP1IWASSU. Accessed July 21, 2017. And http://www.cnn. com/2014/11/06/tech/innovation/foodini-machine-print-food/index. html. Accessed July 21, 2017.

[127] https://www.wildlife.ca.gov/regulations. Accessed July 21, 2017.

[128] The author himself has benefited from this animal research. He was employed at UCLA in the bioscience field and he has been a subject in two clinical trials of drugs for central tremor. These trials resulted from the positive response to the drugs that was exhibited by mice afflicted with similar tremors.

[129] http://www.ada.gov/service_animals_2010.htm. Accessed July 21, 2017.

[130] https://en.m.wikipedia.org/wiki/Pet. Accessed July 21, 2017.

[131] http://www.odditycentral.com/travel/california-town-is-home-to-hundreds-of-free-roaming-wild-peacocks.html. Accessed July 21, 2017.

[132] http://articles.latimes.com/2000/jul/31/local/me-62028. Accessed July 21, 2017.

[133] http://www.bbc.com/future/story/20141014-time-to-put-bugs-on-the-menu. Accessed July 21, 2017.

[134] Weisman, A. (2013). *Countdown, Our last, best hope for a future on earth?*. New York, NY, Boston, MA, London, UK: Little, Brown & Company. pgs3-7.

[135] Coward, H. & Maguire, D. (Eds.). (2000). *Visions Of A New Earth. Religious Perspectives On Population, Consumption, And Ecology.* Albany, NY: State University of New York Press. Ch4.

[136] Norris, G. (1992). *Sharing Silence.* New York, NY: Bell Tower Books. pg39.

[137] www.encyclopediavirginia.org/Inter_caetera_by_Pope_Alexander_VI_May_4_1493. Accessed July 21, 2017.

[138] http://www.roebuckclasses.com/texts/bull/intercaetera1493.html. This domain expired before July 21, 2017.

[139] https://en.wikipedia.org/wiki/Inter_caetera. Accessed July 21, 2017.

[140] Newcomb, S. (2008). *Pagans in the Promised Land, Decoding the Doctrine of Christian Discovery.* Golden, CO: Fulcrum Publishing.

[141] DeFries, R., (2014). *The Big Ratchet. How Humanity Thrives In The Face Of Natural Crises.* New York, NY: Basic Books. pg95.

[142] Weisman, A. (2013). *Countdown, Our last, best hope for a future on earth?.* New York, NY, Boston, MA, London, UK: Little, Brown & Company. pg271.

[143] Ibid., pg275.

[144] www.worldwatch.org/nine-population-strategies-stop-short-9-billion. Accessed July 21, 2017.

[145] https://www.nytimes.com/2017/10/29/opinion/economy-birth-control.html?&moduleDetail=section-news-1&action=click&contentCollection=Opinion&region=Footer&module=MoreInSection&version=WhatsNext&contentID=WhatsNext&pgtype=article. Accessed October 30, 2017.

[146] http://geography.about.com/od/populationgeography/a/onechild.htm. Accessed July 21, 2017.

[147] https://en.wikipedia.org/wiki/One-child_policy. Accessed July 21, 2017.

[148] Fong, M. (2016). *One Child, The Story Of China's Most Radical Experiment.* Boston, MA & New York, NY: Houghton Mifflin Harcourt. pgs213,214.

149 https://en.wikipedia.org/wiki/Demographics_of_Mexico. Accessed July 21, 2017.

150 Gabriela Soto Laveaga, "'Let's become fewer': Soap operas, contraception, and nationalizing the Mexican family in an overpopulated world." *Sexuality Research and Social Policy*. September 2007, vol. 4, no. 3, pgs19–33.

151 http://www.fastcoexist.com/3022073/how-to-defuse-the-population-bomb-soap-operas. Accessed July 21, 2017.

152 Daum, M. (2015). *Selfish, Shallow, And Self-Absorbed. Sixteen Writers On The Decision NOT To Have Kids.* New York, NY: Picador. pg35.

153 Spikins, P. (2015). *How Compassion Made us Human: An Archeology of Stone Age Sentiment.* South Yorkshire S70 2AS, England: Pen and Sword Books Ltd.

154 http://www.nytimes.com/2016/12/19/health/pregnancy-brain-change.html?_r=0. Accessed July 21, 2017. also reported in https://www.theatlantic.com/health/archive/2015/01/what-happens-to-a-womans-brain-when-she-becomes-a-mother/384179/. Accessed July 21, 2017. and in https://www.newscientist.com/article/2116527-becoming-a-mother-may-change-the-brain-to-read-babys-mind/. Accessed July 21, 2017.

155 http://www.npr.org/templates/story/story.php?storyId=7043116. Accessed July 21, 2017. and http://www.npr.org/programs/morning/features/2001/oct/myanmar/011017.myanmar.html. Accessed July 21, 2017.

156 https://themoth.org/stories/the-last-taron. Accessed July 21, 2017. and http://themoth.org/posts/episodes/1301. Accessed July 21, 2017. and http://en.wikipedia.org/wiki/Taron_people. Accessed July 21, 2017. and In his book *Beyond the Last Village* Alan Rabinowitz wrote about the end of the Taron in Myanmar. From pgs 270 and 271:

"We stood outside the church, a one room cabin with a cross carved into its side, watching the scantily clad villagers scurry through the snow. Dawi walked at his usual slow pace, his blackened bare feet in stark contrast to the white snow. … Dawi was the only one of the remaining pure Taron who attended. And the look on his face, while the others sang, clearly indicated that he was there in body alone. … there was nothing that could be done for the Taron, the last remnants of a tribe whose lives had been so pitiful that they had decided to help close the chapter on their own existence. I tried to tell myself that, in the scheme of things, the Taron had taken the best course of action for the well being of future generations. I remained unconvinced."

[157] Daum, M. (2015). *Selfish, Shallow, And Self-Absorbed. Sixteen Writers On The Decision NOT To Have Kids.* New York, NY: Picador.

[158] Buchanan, P. (2002). *The Death of the West, How Dying Populations and Immigrant Invasions Imperil Our Country and Civilization,* New York, NY: St Martin's Press.

[159] According to Wikipedia, https://en.m.wikipedia.org/wiki/Total_fertility_rate. Accessed July 21, 2017. the total fertility rate (TFR), sometimes also called the fertility rate, period total fertility rate (PTFR) or total period fertility rate (TPFR) of a population is the average number of children that would be born to a woman over her lifetime if:

• She was to experience the exact current age-specific fertility rates (ASFRs) throughout her lifetime, and

• She was to survive from birth through the end of her reproductive life. It is obtained by summing the single-year age-specific rates at a given time. The TFR which maintains a stable population is about 2.1 children per woman.

[160] http://vitals.nbcnews.com/_news/2012/07/24/12930475-oopsie-babies-a-third-of-us-births-unintended-study-finds?lite. Accessed July 21, 2017.

[161] http://www.usatoday.com/story/news/nation/militaryintelligence/2014/05/29/birth-rate-teens/9670669/. Accessed July 21, 2017.

[162] http://thenationalcampaign.org/why-it-matters/unplanned-pregnancy Accessed July 21, 2017.

163 Berry, W. (1977, 1996). *The Unsettling Of America, Culture & Agriculture.* San Francisco, CA: Sierra Club Books. from the subsection "Freedom from Fertility" in Chapter 7 of *The Unsettling of America* pg131. or Berry, W. (2002). *The Art Of The Commonplace. The Agrarian Essays Of Wendell Berry.* Berkeley, CA: Counterpoint. pg93.

164 https://en.m.wikipedia.org/wiki/Infanticide_(zoology). Accessed July 21, 2017.

165 https://en.wikipedia.org/wiki/Infanticide. Accessed July 21, 2017.

166 Williamson, Laila (1978). "Infanticide: an anthropological analysis" in Kohl, Marvin. *Infanticide and the Value of Life.* New York, NY: Prometheus Books. pgs61–75.

167 From Native American Pre-Retreat Information, Indian Values etc, Joann Sebastian Morris. See www.zenpeacemakers.org.

168 https://en.m.wikipedia.org/wiki/Infanticide. Accessed July 21, 2017.

169 https://en.wikipedia.org/wiki/Christina_Johansdotter. Accessed July 21, 20178.

170 Perrini, S. (2012). *Baby Farmers of the 19th Century, Women Who Kill.* Published by Goldmineguides.com.

171 Verhagen E, Sauer P.J. (March 2005). "The Groningen Protocol – Euthanasia in Severely Ill Newborns. *New England Journal of Medicine* 352: 959–962. doi:10.1056/NEJMp058026. PMID 15758003. http://www.nejm.org/doi/full/10.1056/NEJMp058026. Accessed July 21, 2017.

172 *"An apology from the BIA". tahtonka (Global Culture, Exploring the Humanities of Humans). 2000. Retrieved 21 February 2010.*

173 *Kevin Gover (2006) [Sep 8, 2000]. Video of Kevin Gover's speech, "Never Again" (Sept. 8, 2000), a formal apology to Native Americans, on behalf of the U.S. Bureau of Indian Affairs (video). U.S. Bureau of Indian Affairs, analog to digital conversion by Harkirat Chawia, Michigan State University, presented by Christopher Buck, Michigan State University.*

[174] *Buck, Christopher (2006). ""Never Again"; Kevin Gover's Apology for the Bureau of Indian Affairs" (PDF). Wicazo SA Review 21 (1 (Spring)): 97–126. JSTOR 4140301. Retrieved Oct 12, 2015.*

[175] http://www.huffingtonpost.com/entry/forgiveness-ceremony-unites-veterans-and-natives-at-standing-rock-casino_us_5845cdb-be4b055b31398b199. Accessed July 21, 2017.

[176] https://www.youtube.com/watch?v=FWU1NBcElSQ. As of July 21, 2017, this content was blocked on copyright grounds.

[177] https://en.m.wikipedia.org/wiki/Genocide_definitions. Accessed July 21, 2017.

[178] https://en.wikipedia.org/wiki/Population_history_of_indigenous_peoples_of_the_Americas. Accessed July 21, 2017.

[179] https://en.wikipedia.org/wiki/Armenian_Genocide. Accessed July 21, 2017.

[180] https://en.wikipedia.org/wiki/The_Holocaust. Accessed July 21, 2017.

[181] https://en.wikipedia.org/wiki/1971_Bangladesh_genocide. Accessed July 21, 2017.

[182] https://en.wikipedia.org/wiki/Cambodian_genocide. Accessed July 21, 2017.

[183] https://en.wikipedia.org/wiki/Kurdish_genocide. Accessed July 21, 2017.

[184] https://en.wikipedia.org/wiki/Rwandan_genocide. Accessed July 21, 2017.

[185] https://en.wikipedia.org/wiki/Bosnian_genocide. Accessed July 21, 2017.

[186] https://en.m.wikipedia.org/wiki/Humayun_Khan_(soldier). Accessed July 21, 2017.

[187] Dorn, H., 1962, as recorded in Cohen, J., pg237.

[188] Cohen, J. (1995). *How Many People Can the Earth Support?* New York, NY: W. W. Norton & Co. pg161.

[189] Estimates of 300 and 1000 billion were thrown out as being beyond common sense.

[190] Silverstein, Shel. (1964). *The Giving Tree*, New York, NY: Harper & Row.

[191] For a discussion of deep-time see Chapter 8 of *Active Hope* by Joanna Macy and Chris Johnstone.

[192] From a conversation between an elderly, semi-lucid hospital patient and the author.

[193] Pamela Teagarden in Forbes Quote of the Day, Saturday, February 4, 2017.

[194] Berry, W. (1998). *A Timbered Choir*. Berkeley, CA: Counterpoint Press.

[195] Sometimes strengths are just loose canons looking for a target.

[196] http://www.nytimes.com/2015/12/13/world/europe/climate-change-accord-paris.html?_r=0. Accessed July 22, 2017.

[197] http://www.nytimes.com/interactive/projects/cp/climate/2015-paris-climate-talks/key-points-of-the-final-paris-climate-draft?action=click&contentCollection=2015-paris-climate-talks&module=g-series-graphic. Accessed July 22, 2017.

[198] Barrows, A & Macy, J. (Trans.). (1996). *Rilke's Book of Hours, Love Poems to God*. New York, NY: Riverhead Books.

[199] Daly, H. & Cobb, J. (1989). *For The Common Good, Redirecting The Economy Toward Community, The Environment, And A Sustainable Future*. Boston, MA: Beacon Press. pg39.

[200] http://www.newyorker.com/magazine/2016/04/18/a-radical-attempt-to-save-the-reefs-and-forests. Accessed July 22, 2017. This issue also said: These practices of gene manipulation are simply an acceleration of Man's practice of selective breeding. The caution is that the new techniques give a power that accelerates results far beyond our capability to predict. ...

In Man's case, nature has pruned the tree of human emergence through death and disappearance. Homo Sapiens is just the last twig bearing any fruit.

201 http://www.nytimes.com/2015/11/15/magazine/the-crispr-quandary. html?_r=0. Accessed July 22, 2017.

202 https://www.washingtonpost.com/news/morning-mix/ wp/2017/01/24/biologists-breed-life-form-with-lab-made-dna-dont-call-it-jurassic-park/?utm_term=.d68ce9beb929. Accessed July 22, 2017.

203 https://www.nytimes.com/2015/10/20/science/editing-of-pig-dna-may-lead-to-more-organs-for-people.html?_r=0. Accessed July 22, 2017.

204 http://www.cnn.com/2016/12/15/health/babies-three-people-embryos/index.html. Accessed July 22, 2017.

205 http://www.theverge.com/a/verge-2021/jennifer-doudna-crispr-gene-editing-healthcare. Accessed July 22, 2017.

206 Weisman, A. (2013). *Countdown, Our last, best hope for a future on earth?*. New York, NY, Boston, MA, London, UK: Little, Brown & Company.

207 It could also be argued that if God really wanted to, He could find a way around the contraceptive. Although I've had a granddaughter while her mother was on the pill, I won't attempt that argument here.

208 Berry, W. (2002). *The Art Of The Commonplace. The Agrarian Essays Of Wendell Berry*. Berkeley, CA: Counterpoint. pg126.

209 https://www.youtube.com/watch?v=5TMFTEPJzOU&feature=youtu.be. Accessed July 22, 2017. About 6 minutes, 10 seconds into the interview.

210 Jackson, T. (2009). *Prosperity Without Growth, Economics for a Finite Planet*. United Kingdom: earthscan. and Kallis, G. (2010). *In Defense Of Degrowth*. Ecological Economics www.elsevier.com/locate/ecolecon. Elsevier.

211 https://www.degrowth.info/en/what-is-degrowth/. Accessed July, 2017.

212 http://www.degrowth.de/en/. Accessed July 22, 2017.

213 From a PBS NewsHour segment of October 22, 2016 titled Will South Korea's robot revolution hurt American jobs?

214 Ford, M. (2015). *Rise of the Robots, Technology and the Threat of a Jobless Future.* New York, NY: Basic Books. pg252.

215 Ibid., p281.

216 Ibid. From praise for Rise of the Robots by ZDNet.

217 https://www.theguardian.com/technology/2017/jan/05/japanese-company-replaces-office-workers-artificial-intelligence-ai-fukoku-mutual-life-insurance. Accessed July 22, 2017.

218 https://www.technologyreview.com/s/603381/ai-software-learns-to-make-ai-software/. Accessed July 22, 2017.

219 http://money.cnn.com/2017/01/26/technology/kill-switch-ai-ethics/index.html. Accessed July 22, 2017.

220 http://www.msn.com/en-us/money/companies/amazon-is-piloting-teams-with-a-30-hour-workweek/ar-BBw5T8N?OCID=ansmsnnews11. Accessed July 22, 2017.

221 http://fortune.com/2016/08/28/amazon-tests-30-hour-work-week/ Accessed July 22, 2017.

222 Victor Davis Hanson, Los Angeles Times, July 9, 2017, pg A17.

223 Berry, W. (1990, 2010). *What Are People For?* Berkeley, CA: Counterpoint. pg 10.

224 http://www.cnbc.com/2016/08/03/trump-asks-why-us-cant-use-nukes-msnbcs-joe-scarborough-reports.html. Accessed July 22, 2017.

225 Fong, M. (2016). *One Child, The Story Of China's Most Radical Experiment.* Boston, MA & New York, NY: Houghton Mifflin Harcourt. pg209.

226 https://en.wikipedia.org/wiki/List_of_cities_by_population_density. Accessed July 22, 2017. and https://simple.wikipedia.org/wiki/List_of_ countries_by_population_density. Accessed July 22, 2017.

227 https://www.cia.gov/library/publications/resources/the-world-fact-book/geos/gm.html. Accessed July 22, 2017.

228 http://www.npr.org/2016/08/28/491726848/activists-consider-the-cli-mate-impact-of-having-children. Accessed July 22, 2017. August 28, 2016 5:10 PM ET, Ferorelli and Kallman are co-founders of conceivablefutures. org, a women-led network of Americans bringing awareness to the threat climate change poses to reproductive justice, and demanding an end to US fossil fuel subsidies.

229 http://www.forbes.com/sites/patrickmoorhead/2016/10/17/qual-comm-unveils-the-worlds-first-5g-modem-snapdragon-x50-for-28-ghz-mmwave-networks/#7fbbcd7e3896. Accessed July 22, 2017.

230 Casteneda, C. (1974). *Tales of Power*. New York, NY: Simon and Schuster.